Mounting Your Your Deer Head

AT HOME

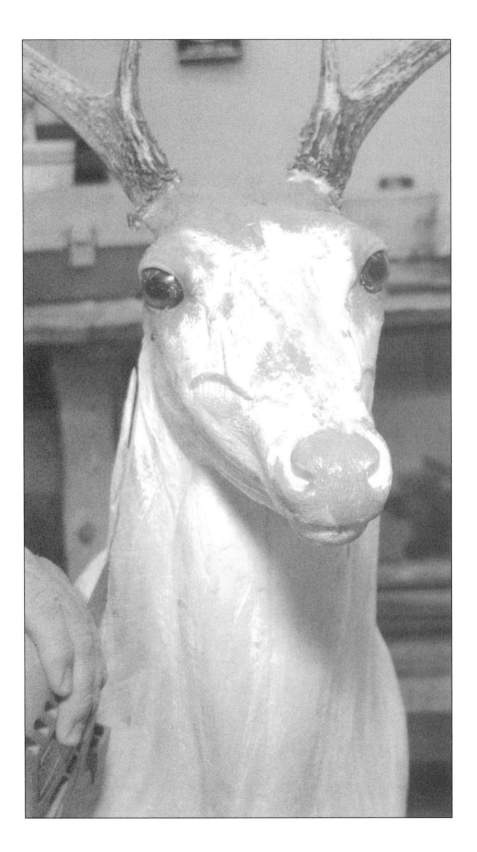

OUTDOORSMAN'S EDGE®

Mounting Your Your Deer Head

AT HOME

Monte Burch

Front cover image: Monte Burch
All images by author unless noted otherwise.

Published by: Woods N' Water, Inc.
Peter and Kate Fiduccia
P.O. Box 550
Florida, NY 10921

Printed in the United States of America
10 9 8 7 6 5 4 3 2 1
ISBN: 0-9722804-8-0

TABLE OF CONTENTS

ACKNOWLEDGEMENTS

Many thanks to Mark Nash,
an excellent taxidermist, outdoor writer and friend,
for all his help with this book.
Shown here is an example of some of his work.

INTRODUCTION

Taxidermy, or mounting game heads such as deer is fun, instructive, a great way of displaying your trophies, and can often lead to a hobby that can turn into a home money maker. Learning to mount your own deer head at home is fairly simple, especially with today's materials and tactics. It does take time, patience, and attention to detail. With the instructions, photos, and illustrations in this book, even a first-timer can create a trophy mount of which they can be proud. The trick to making this easy work is to take the chore in steps. So, the book is written in this manner, stopping places between the steps. The best tactic is to first read the book thoroughly to understand the overall process. Then, order the materials and do the preliminary work needed. After this, you can take each section step-by-step as you more thoroughly understand the process. In addition to traditional taxidermy techniques, European style mounts, mounting boards, and even novelty deer items are also included. Have fun!

—Monte Burch

SECTION I
Tools and Materials

1
Tools

Although it's possible to mount a deer head with only a handful of tools, a number of specialty tools can make the chore easier. These special tools can also help produce a better quality mount.

THE WORKPLACE

You can work on your kitchen table, a workbench in your garage or shop, or even a card table temporarily set up for the task—as long as you have a good solid work surface that's easy to clean. A plastic laminate

Having a good, convenient workplace is important for doing taxidermy work, such as deer-head mounting. It's a good idea to have a separate room or, better yet, a separate building that can be kept locked.

top is an excellent choice, and a stainless steel surface is ideal, since it can be washed easily and won't scratch or mar as badly as does the plastic laminate.

Regardless of the surface, the worktable or bench should be sturdy, and at a comfortable height to suit your stature and working preference. For instance, will you be sitting at a bench, on a chair or stool, or will you be standing for the most part? Stooping over a too-low

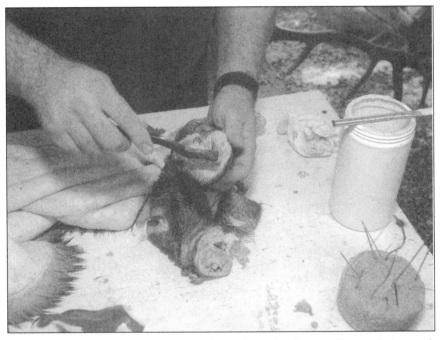

Work surfaces should be at a comfortable height, either for standing or sitting, and should be easy to clean.

surface can make for painful backaches. A good, solid-metal vise and even a tiltable craft vise can be very helpful. You'll also want cabinets to hold tools and materials, and they should be lockable if children have access to the area. Many of the tools you'll be using are sharp, and many of the materials are toxic.

If possible, the workplace should be separate from other activity areas. Taxidermy does have its own "aroma," and some folks may not appreciate it. Your best choice is a room that can be cooled and/or heated, and has good ventilation. That's a vital consideration due to the materials being handled. A source of water can also be handy for clean-up and strong lighting is necessary. A north window will provide excellent daytime illumination, but you'll also need overhead lighting.

For those who get serious about taxidermy, the "out-back" shop is a tradition. Just make sure it closes tightly to prevent children, pets, and wild animals from getting in. A stray cat can make short work of what took you hours. You will also need a freezer to hold capes until you're ready to work them. For the individual who simply wants to tan his own trophy, a simple basement corner will suffice, and you can

Lockable cabinets should be available to keep materials and tools safely out of reach from children and pets.

use the family freezer, as long as the capes are well marked, and you have room for them.

KNIVES

You simply can't have enough knives. At least that's how many of us feel. Field skinning knives with a rounded point and gut hook are excellent for general purpose, in-the-field caping and skinning. For most final caping, however, smaller, short-

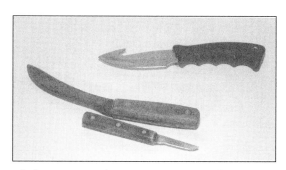

It's important to have an assortment of knives on hand, including general-purpose skinning as well as short-bladed knives for caping.

bladed, thin-handled knives are best. A leatherworker's or taxidermist's knife is a good choice, but any number of small fixed-blade knives may also be useful. Add a sharp-pointed blade knife and a skiving knife to the list, and a fish-skinning knife with a serrated blade, which can be used to rough-up the hide for better adhesion when gluing.

FLESHING AND THINNING TOOLS

Special knives are needed for fleshing, including the draw-knife type for the heavy-duty fleshing of the neck and most of the cape. But although a draw-knife works quite well, the better quality fleshing knives have both a sharp and dull side for more versatile use. The smaller Jim-Hall type fleshers can be used for reaching into tight places, and paint scrapers can be ground into small "fleshers" for getting into a variety of small spots.

Fleshing and thinning tools are essential. A drawknife or specially designed fleshing knives make the chore easier, although large hunting knives can also be used.

You'll also need a floor- or bench-mounted fleshing beam for fleshing the cape. The bench model is fairly easy to make from a two-by-six. Round the end with a saber or band saw, then use a draw knife or belt sander to remove the square top edge. You can make your own floor model just as simply.

A fleshing beam is necessary, and a floor model works well.

Or you can make up a board that can be fastened to the top of a workbench.

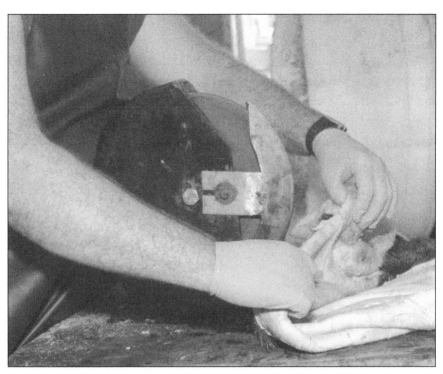

Powered fleshing machines can be used for thinning hides.

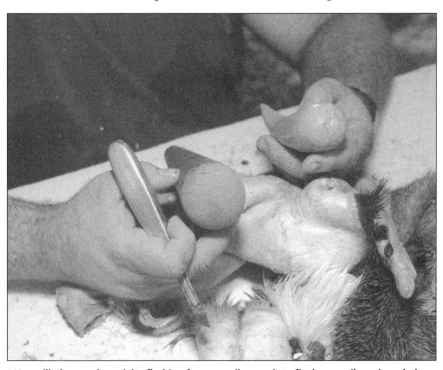

You will also need specialty fleshing forms small enough to fit the nostrils and eye holes.

If you become serious about doing your own deer-head mounts, you'll probably want to acquire a powered fleshing machine that will thin and flesh the cape in much less time than you can do it by hand, making a tedious chore much easier and quicker. (FYI, new models can cost several hundred dollars.) A couple of other tools can further

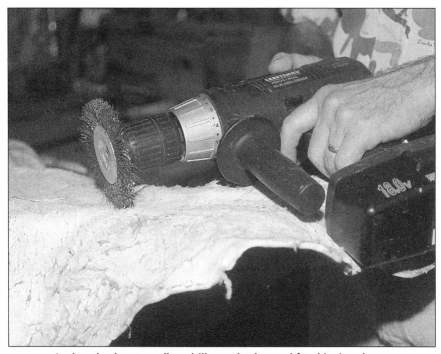

A wire wheel on a cordless drill can also be used for thinning chores.

Knife sharpeners are extremely important. Keep simple hand-held models nearby your workbench for quick and easy touch-ups.

simplify fleshing with a machine: Shaped wooden pieces that can be pushed through the eye and nostril holes to keep the skin taut during fleshing and thinning operations, and a wire wheel on an electric motor or, better yet, mounted on a cordless electric drill can also be handy. And a good scalpel and plenty of blades are indispensable for detailed fleshing around eyes, ears, and nose.

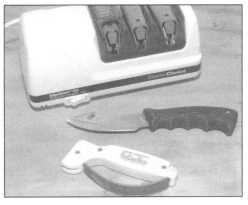

Quality knife sharpeners are also important, since a dull knife is worse than useless when it comes to taxidermy. One slip and you can

Powered models make quick work of sharpening a number of knives.

ruin hours of work. Among the best sharpeners I've tested are the AccuSharp® and Chef's Choice®. The latter has a diamond electric hone that sharpens blades instantly and consistently.

Finally, you'll need woodworking tools if you desire to make your own mounting boards—including a band saw, a router, and a good sander.

SPECIALTY TOOLS

You can acquire a wide variety of useful specialty tools at craft stores and taxidermy supply houses. Modeling tools are needed for sculpting clay around the head form, and an ear opener makes this tedious chore easier. Wood rasps and rifflers of several sizes can be used to sculpt the urethane foam head forms. A farrier's rasp, for example, has large, well-spaced teeth and makes quick work of form shaping, while a Stout Ruffer is made especially to quickly prepare the form for

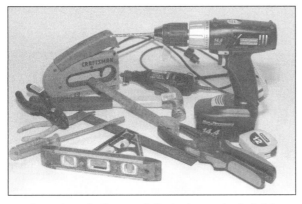

A number of other specialty tools are also helpful.

hide glue without damaging details. You'll need forceps, surgical scissors, surgical gloves, calipers, T-pins, brad drivers, an electric glue gun, an electric drill with bits and screwdriver blades, plus a variety of needles, including cutting and cape and hide needles, as well as glover's or suture needles. An ordinary fine-point carpenter's saw can be used for cutting skull plates and other bone chores, but it

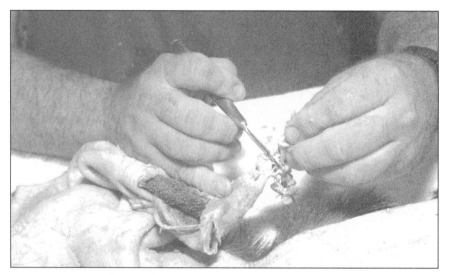

A sharp scalpel and spare blades will be invaluable.

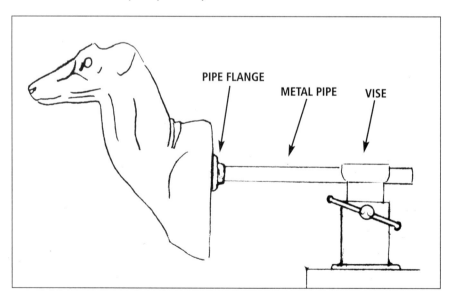

You'll need some method of holding the form steady for working. A pipe with flange clamped in a sturdy vise is one possibility.

A mounting stand makes the chore easier. These can be purchased, or you can make your own.

dulls quickly. A hacksaw can also be used, a butcher's saw is better, but the best is a taxidermist's bone saw. It doesn't dull as quickly and the fine teeth cut rapidly and smoothly. A powered saw, such as the Black & Decker handsaw/jigsaw, can make short work of any bone- or manikin-cutting chores. A staple gun can be used to attach the hide to the backboard, a tumbler

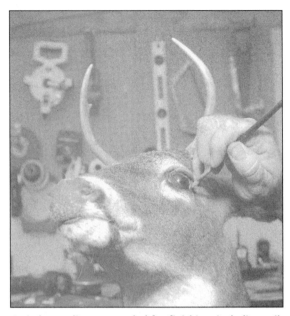

Artist's supplies are needed for finishing, including oil colors and a variety of brushes.

is handy for drying capes after washing, pickling or tanning, and a Dremel motor tool with accessories can be valuable for some detailing jobs, such as veining.

One of the handiest tools is a mounting stand to hold the head form while you work on it. Commercial models are available, or you can make your own if you're handy with a welder. They can be floor or bench mounted; they are also tiltable and adjustable in height to allow for a variety of positions. If you have more than one head working at a time, a series of mounting brackets to hold several heads can be extremely handy.

You will need buckets and tubs, measuring cups, and scales for tanning the capes. You will also need artist's supplies, including acrylic or oil-based paints for the nose and eyes, as well as brushes to apply the color. Many professionals use air brushes for these chores, but the initial cost, of course, is more.

Calipers and a cloth or seamstress tape measure are essential for taking important circumference and other measurements. You'll also want a regular, twelve-foot carpenter's tape measure and a small carpenter's bubble level for setting the manikin level and placing the eyes. Make sure you wear rubber or latex gloves during the initial

If you do any amount of skinning, make sure you have a good, sturdy meat pole, gambrels, and a means of hoisting the carcass

caping or skinning, tongue depressors to mix materials, combs, including furriers combs, stiff bristle brushes, old toothbrushes and small paint brushes, plus modeling tools and sandpaper or sanding screens to rough up the form before applying glue.

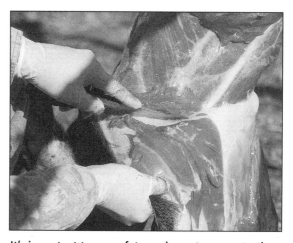

It's important to use safety equipment: eye protection, a dust mask, a rubber apron, and lots of disposable rubber gloves.

Other basic hand tools include pliers, hammers, and screwdrivers, including one large flat-bladed driver. (I have one I've bent slightly on the end and it's perfect for working the skin away from the antler bases.) And, of course, your safety equipment should include eye protection, dust masks, a rubber apron, and plenty of disposable rubber gloves.

2
Materials

A variety of materials are needed to create a deer-head mount, and you can purchase them separately or buy a kit, such as Van Dyke's Deer Mounting Kit, a good choice for beginners. It contains all the materials you'll need at a very economical price, including a quality polyurethane head form, eyes, eye clay, ear forms, the necessary tanning materials, mounting and finishing materials, along with complete instructions. As you become more proficient, you'll probably desire to increase both your tools and materials selection.

HEAD FORMS

In days past, taxidermists had to build their own forms. One of my earliest home references was a very old copy of Lessons in Taxidermy by Prof. J.W. Elwood, B.S., published by the Northwestern School of Taxidermy. I don't know how old the lesson pamphlets are,

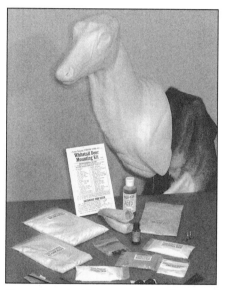

If you're starting your first deer-head mount, consider using a mounting kit that contains all the materials needed to mount one deer head. (PHOTO COURTESY WASCO)

The Van Dyke Kit is another excellent choice. It is available with a wide selection of forms.

but instructions are given for

using papier-mâché as well as constructing your own maché forms. Today's taxidermists have it much, much easier with polyurethane molded head forms that are not only ready to use at a reasonable price, but also available in a wide variety of poses and sizes. Some are even sculpted to match regional deer characteristics, and they're extremely anatomically realistic, complete with muscling and veining details.

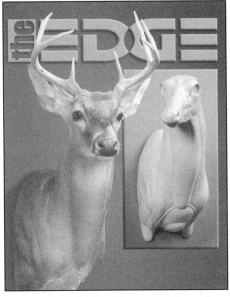

Having the right form is a must. These days, a wide variety of polyurethane deer-head and even full-body and half-body forms are available. (PHOTO COURTESY WASCO)

It is important to choose not only the correct-size head form, but also the regional model and pose, whether you desire upright, sneak, left turn, right turn and so forth. (Note: This chapter refers mainly to whitetail mounts, but many taxidermy supply houses carry mule-deer manikins as well.) Following are some typical forms available from Van Dyke's Taxidermy Supply:

Their number-one selling form is the WT Series, an all-around form sculpted to fit deer from across the United States, from the mideastern region to the upper southern tier and the far Midwestern states. They're available in fifty-four sizes in right-turn upright,

Today's sculpted forms are extremely detailed, and many are designed for deer from specific regions. (PHOTO COURTESY WASCO)

straight upright, left-turn upright, right-turn droop, straight droop, and left-turn droop poses. The WTOS, or Whitetail Offset Shoulder Series, is also designed to match a broad range of deer, yet with a style that is unique. Fourteen WTOS sizes include right-turn sneak, left-turn sneak, straight sneak, right-turn straight offset and left-turn straight offset.

In 1999, Don Holt sculpted their offset shoulder sweep design, which quickly became their best-selling deer form of that year. It continues to be very popular and is available in left-turn, upright sweep, right-turn upright sweep, left-turn droop and right-turn droop. Holt's Lone Star Collection designs were taken from whitetail deer in the Texas Hill Country. These deer tend to have a smaller face, more petite skeletal structure, and a more slender neck and shoulder area. These same forms are often used by taxidermists for early season bow-killed deer from the upper New England states and along the southeastern coast.

Forms come in a wide variety of sizes, and it's important that you correctly match the form to the cape being mounted. (PHOTO COURTESY WASCO)

The Don Holt Wall Pedestal Roman Nose Series is a more relaxed design with features that show little fear or threat. The Pedestal and Specialty Series requires more forethought and work than the standard upright pose. As there is considerably more shoulder, you must always leave more cape to cover the extended area. Also, you should decide if you are going to finish the back and what type of material you want to use. Some taxidermists choose to cover the area with extra hide; others use leather or felt.

The Legacy Series forms sculpted by Scott Lennard are designed for deer in the northern part of the country. These manikins have the larger features so prevalent in deer north of the Mason/Dixon Line.

Aaron Connelly's Bantley Series has thirty-eight styles and models of eastern and northeastern deer in every upright pose, incorporating the characteristic broad, muscular brisket, extremely full shoulder, long neck, and slender nose. These forms are perfect for early-bow and black-powder deer and younger bucks that haven't bulked up yet.

The upright, thick neck and shoulder of Van Dyke's Classics manikins were developed for those whitetails taken during the heavy rut in the midwest, east, and south. The proud stance indicates the wariness of a fully alert whitetail deer, its lower jaw line well above the top of the shoulder, the side angle of the face semi-parallel to the ground, and, in most cases, both ears directed forward to indicate the buck's high sense of awareness. The head is pulled back sharply, but still allows wall clearance for antlers.

The sneak pose is normal for whitetail deer that have been made aware of danger. They will lower their heads until the lower jaw is equal to or below the top of their shoulders. The angle of the head will be parallel to the ground and the ears will be twisting in a very active range of motions to pick up suspicious sounds.

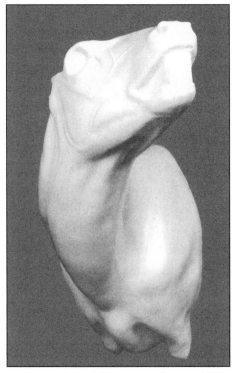

Manikins are also available in a variety of specialty poses, including full-sweep left or right turns and fighting bucks in both turns, so two bucks can be mounted in a fighting position. Grooming and browsing buck forms are also available.

The Bob Snow Coues Series forms are designed specifically for the tiny deer, using references from those areas of the U.S. they inhabit. The same small forms can be used for very small deer taken

Open-mouth manikins are also available through many suppliers. (PHOTO COURTESY WASCO)

along the coastal areas of Florida, Georgia, and the Carolinas.

For the really ambitious craftsman, a number of full-body forms are also available for fawn, doe, and buck. Forms come in a variety of poses, including lying down, standing, walking, running, jumping, and even foot stomping.

Dan Chase Taxidermy Supply Company carries literally hundreds of manikins in a wide variety of poses—E-Z Mount forms that include several pedestal styles, which have become increasingly popular. Half forms, with deer standing or jumping, are also very much in demand and provide a most unusual mount, as will turn-around and browsing manikins, which are also available.

John Rinehart Taxidermy Company, now a McKenzie Company, has a line of manikins called Final Generation that are extremely easy for first-timers to use. They feature Final Generation's patented Brain Ridge, which was specially designed for ease and efficiency in mounting antlers. Just cut the antler base to fit over the Brain Ridge and screw the antlers to the manikin.

These manikins also feature Beautiful Eyes Eye-Rite II®, a patented process that provides a detailed, anatomically correct pre-set eye, eliminating the one problem most beginners have. Pre-set eyes dry exactly the way they are placed, unlike eyes set in clay, which tend to move while they are drying as the moisture from within the clay, trapped under the skin, is released through the drying hide. The wet clay rehydrates the hide, which means you must dry it again, a drying and rehydrating sequence that will occur numerous times when eyes are set with clay. You have to continually check the eyes as they dry, making adjustments as the skin around them moves and distorts. With pre-set eyes there is no moisture to release and cause deformities.

Rinehart offers Flehmen Whitetail manikins, which can be used with their teeth and tongue insets to re-create this unusual look, and several other open-mouth mounts are also available. Rinehart also offers Speed Septum, a fast and innovative way of re-creating the translucent membrane between the nostrils of a deer. You may want to apply Derma Coat Nose/Hoof Clear to the nose to create a very realistic "wet" look.

Another interesting project to consider is mounting shed antlers, and there are a number of shed-connection devices available to allow

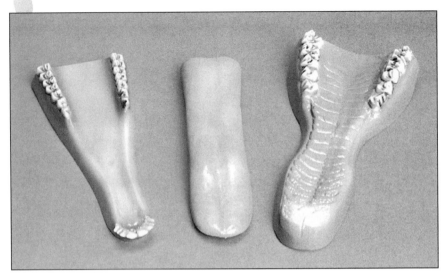

Tongue and teeth sets are available for open-mouth mounts. (PHOTO COURTESY WASCO)

you to mount sheds to a manikin. You can then use a cape salvaged from another deer for finishing the mounting.

TANNING CHEMICALS

A wide variety of chemicals can be used to tan capes for mounting, and once again, they can be purchased in kit form or separately from companies like WASCO, Van Dyke's, and Rinehart.

The Tan'um Kit™ contains traditional ammonium alum tanning materials: ten pounds ammonium alum, four pounds pickling crystals, one quart of Protal Tanning oil and eight ounces of sodium bicarbonate. Note that tanning also requires salt, which this kit does not furnish. The Curatan Kit® is excellent for light skins. It comes with one quart Curatan, two pounds pickling crystals and four ounces sodium bicarbonate. The Lutan® F Kit 100, which contains twelve pounds of Lutan F, eight ounces sodium bicarbonate, one quart Protal and eight pounds of pickling crystals, will tan one hundred pounds of dry weight hides.

The Syn-Oil Kit is one of the easiest home-tanning kits on the market. It contains ten pounds Tannium, eight ounces sodium bicarbonate, one quart Protal and two pounds of Oxalic acid, and requires twenty pounds of salt. Syn-Oil Tan is a synthetic agent that tans very deep to produce a durable, long-lasting, perfectly tanned cape every time. This kit comes with Bruce Rittel's new Safe-Tee

Acid for the pickling and includes enough chemicals to tan four average-sized deer capes. You can also try Rittel's EZ-2000 Kit. It uses their own EZ 100 powdered Syntan Tanning agent that eliminates environmental and personal handling problems. The tanned capes are durable and stretchy.

The Van Dyke's chart shown illustrates the different chemicals and the tanning results for those of you who opt to purchase individual tanning agents and materials instead of buying a kit.

You'll also need to acquire chemicals for the pickling process. The common acids traditionally used for pickling include oxalic, formic, citric and sulfuric—not only very dangerous to have around the shop, but in some cases difficult to ship or obtain.

Van Dyke's Pickling Crystals work equally well, yet they are thoroughly safe and present no health hazards. Bruce Rittel's Safe-Tee Acid is rapidly replacing all other acids for pickling processes. There is no hazardous shipping fee, it's safe enough to handle without protective equipment and there is no problem disposing of the pickle; it may be poured right down the drain. But the most important benefit is the acid/pickle produces a very plump, white hide.

You will need tester strips for determining pickle-solution pH, and sodium bicarbonate to neutralize the acids. Cleaner/degreasers and blood removal products are handy, as are bactericides such as Bruce Rittel's PS-650, which will prevent the loss of any cape or hide due to bacteria or fungus.

A tanning oil is also needed to create a stretchy cape that is easily mounted, and I would recommend Bee Natural Pro-Carve Tanning Oil Additive for getting leather to stretch and stay where you want it. Pro-Carve not only allows the stretch you need, it makes working with

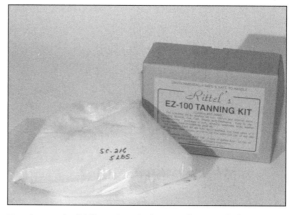

Tanning and pickling chemicals are also needed. You can purchase kits that include everything except salt, or you can buy tanning agents and pickling chemicals individually.

leather a much simpler job, especially in the thin areas around the eyes, nose and ears. Bee Natural North Country Tanning Oil doesn't leave any residue on the hide and accepts glue readily, aiding in the exact placement of critical parts. Another excellent oil, Rittel's Pro Plus Oil is used one part Pro Plus Oil to two parts hot tap water—a great choice for mounts.

Antler stain and wax can also add to the looks of your mount, and if you intend to do European-style mounts, you'll also need basic beautician's white and 40 volume hydrogen peroxide as well as Bruce Rittel's Kilzodor, odor eliminator, an organic, biodegradable, non-flammable chemical.

GLUES AND ADHESIVES

A wide variety of glues and adhesives can be used for the various chores of attaching the hide to the form. Van Dyke's Form Paste is a slow-drying dextrine-based glue designed to be effective across a broad range of temperatures and humidity. It also works well with instant preservatives. Hidemaster is an extremely strong, concentrated epoxy glue. Hide, Skin & Ear Paste is a multi-use product that sticks to any plastic, hide, or skin, gives the craftsman plenty of working time and cleans up with soap and water. "Real Ears" by Tecnaglu is an ear liner adhesive designed specifically to help the whitetail taxidermist create realistic ears with no extra finish work. AFG Hide Paste is a premixed substance that tacks up within hours, eliminating the process of having to go back hours and days later to re-press the hide into depressions. Van Dyke's also carries a line of professional epoxy products such as KEYpoxy Hide & Skin, KEY Ear-Epox and Sculp-Epox modeling compound.

WASCO carries a full line of hide paste supplies, including Eco-Grip Hide Paste, Latex Hide Paste, Hidemaster Epoxy Hidepaste, Killer Glue Epoxy Hidepaste, WASCO Hide Paste and Sallie Dahmes Hide Paste. Rinehart's EPO-Grip hide adhesive cures in four to six hours, won't sag or run, and can be used with tanned or dry-preserved hides.

For building up the form around ear butts, eyes, and other areas, you'll need modeling compounds such as Aves Apoxie® Clay , which has great plasticity and handling features that make it very user friendly. It is a two-part product that has the advantage of no shrinkage and simple water clean-up. Critter Clay™ is a lightweight, non-shrinking, non-toxic clay great for detail work. All-Game® from Van Dyke's, a taxidermy standard for years, can be mixed with water or mineral spirits to smooth the mixture to a feather edge. WASCO carries WASCO clay, Apoxie Clay, Critter Clay, and Sallie Dames Ear Base materials.

You'll need adhesives for gluing in ear forms and for gluing the hide to the form. (PHOTO COURTESY WASCO)

OTHER MATERIALS AND SUPPLIES

If you don't buy a kit for mounting a deer head, and you need to purchase supplies and materials separately, be aware that quality glass eyes rank among the most important purchases. They're available in sizes ranging from

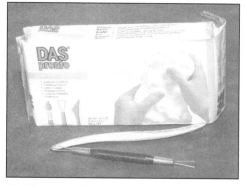

Taxidermist's clay or modeling clay is required for modeling the form.

28mm up to 36mm to fit different animal sizes. Van Dyke's Natural Eyes™ feature soft, marbleized veining blended with accurate colorations and a white scleral band that contains realistic red veins at the corners of each eye. Their Pre-Rotated Natural Eyes Series use a patented system for that distinctive look, and to add even more authenticity, Nictitating Membrane Eyes are available in all Dan Rinehart "pre-Molded" eye Deer manikins, along with their nictitating membrane reference. This revolutionary method allows you to re-create the whitetail's eye, including the entire tear duct, with great realism.

You will also need ear liners, which are available in several different sizes and materials, including traditional fabric and plastic.

Van Dyke's Natural Ears™ come in small, medium and large, and feature detailed veining. Completely anatomically accurate, these integrated ears are extremely flexible and are available in an alert forward position.

Van Dyke's KEY Ear-Epox is a specially formulated resin designed for use with plastic ear liners—a mixed, two-part epoxy that bonds easily to damp skin or leather, ending the problem of ear drumming and drastically reducing your working time. When you're ready to start this phase of your mount, clean the inside of the ear with lacquer thinner or acetone

Eyes may come with certain manikins. In other cases, you'll have to purchase them separately. They're available in a variety of qualities and sizes. (PHOTO COURTESY WASCO)

to remove any oily residue, then thoroughly rough up the ears using a Stout Ruffer. Mix the KEY Ear-Epox and apply to both sides of the ear liner. Remove any materials that may have gotten in or onto the hair with lacquer thinner, then adjust the skin of the ear to the ear liner.

Waxed cape sewing thread is often used for sewing up the capes. These days, however, Spiderwire, braided fishing line, is the choice of many taxidermists.

Since salt is essential, ordinary stock salt, available in fifty pound bags, is the most economical you can buy. Borax and alum, used for some processes, are available at garden supply stores, the latter in the form of aluminum sulfate. Other practical supplies include No. 4

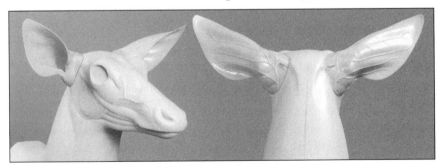

Ear liners can be purchased in different sizes and materials. Many of today's plastic ear liners feature veining for more realism. WASCO carries a full line of ear bases, including the Brad Eppley series and Ear-Tech bases. (PHOTO COURTESY WASCO)

finish and No. 2 shingle nails as well as self-starting wood screws, beeswax, turpentine, instant-bonding glue to seal up tiny, hard-to-sew holes or slits, hair-setting gel for smoothing down unruly hairs and paints, either acrylic or oil colors, for air-brushing or hand-painting the finishing details.

GAME HEAD PANELS

Deer heads are often mounted on wooden plaques or panels which can be purchased or made quite easily if you have the woodworking tools and a little experience. The panels can be simple or ornate, with

You may wish to mount the heads on decorative panels. Choose from the wide variety on the market, or make your own. (PHOTO COURTESY WASCO)

carved or routed designs. Either way, whether you decide on wooden plaques or form boards without plaques, you'll need metal hangers to display your mount.

Visual References and Measurements

Realistic mounting of deer heads requires knowledge of how the animal should appear, as well as precise measurements of the deer carcass in order to obtain the correct manikin.

3
Visual References

Any experienced taxidermist will say you just can't get enough reference material. The more you can obtain, the better your chances of producing a realistic mount. A wide variety of sources are available, including both two- and three-dimensional references and, ideally, close-up photos of live deer from magazines and books and photos of other taxidermists' mounts. You can also learn a great deal by attending taxidermist competitions and shows, where you can study other mounts. Be careful in using photos and information garnered at exhibitions because you may repeat the mistakes that other taxidermists have made. They can, however, give you an excellent idea of "where to start," helping you decide what type of manikin would look best with your trophy and which pose you would like.

Another smart tactic these days is to utilize a digital

Good visual references are a must for quality taxidermy work. A wide range of one-dimensional photos and three-dimensional forms are available.

You can learn a lot by studying the work of other good taxidermists. The above photos are from Bass Pro's Traveling Whitetail Exhibition, Legendary Whitetails. If you get a chance to see these mounts in person, don't hesitate.

camera to photograph the game head you intend to mount from different angles before the head is skinned.

The following series of photos were taken at the Bass Pro "Legendary Whitetails" traveling whitetail exhibition—an array of mounts well worth seeing if you get the opportunity. A permanent exhibit is also on display in the Wonders of Wildlife Zooquarium located next door to Bass Pro Shops' Outdoor World in Springfield, Missouri. A visit here is a priceless learning experience for any taxidermist.

The single best reference source, however, is live deer you can study and photograph, and I'm not referring to sitting in a tree stand and shooting snapshots. My good friend Mark Nash, who helped a great deal with this book, keeps live deer. As he pointed out on one visit while a doe licked his hand, "See the color detail in the nose. You really can't understand that without spending time studying live deer."

If you don't have live deer of your own, go to a game farm or zoo that has whitetails. Take extremely tight close-ups of the animals in a variety of poses and, preferably, during spring, summer, fall, and winter so that you have an idea of the differences in the body and coloring the animals display in these time periods. Of course, you'll be most interested in photographing in the fall, or when bucks are at their peak. It's important to use a telephoto lens and get extremely tight close-ups of the eyes, ears, nose, and lips, the most worrisome trouble spots for many beginning taxidermists. Be sure to take photos from as many angles as possible, capturing all the details visible from above, below, in front, and from the back. Also note that one of the main problems with using game-farm deer is that they often have more of a "relaxed" look than a super-wary alertness, so it is important to get some photos of wild deer as well.

Compile a card file or notebook of three-by-five photos detailing each portion of the deer head and keep the picture file near your work area for quick reference.

Close-up photos of live deer, especially eyes, nose, and ears, are indispensable. The above images are by Mark Nash, professional taxidermist and wildlife photographer. (PHOTOS COURTESY MARK NASH)

Commercial reference forms are also available from taxidermist supply houses.

DEATH MASKS

Professional taxidermists often make "death masks" or study casts of the animals. This is especially important in work for competition, but it can also be used as a reference for mounting heads at home as well. Study casts fall into three categories: skin casts, which have the skin left on; carcass casts, made after the head has been skinned; and slip casts, in which the skin is left on, but the hair is shaved off. The latter two types reveal musculature, while the former recreates the exact anatomy: hair over muscles. Animal sculptures often use carcass and slip casts, but skin casts are normally the best for those who wish to expand their knowledge of anatomy for deer-head mounting purposes.

You won't want to make a death mask of a head you intend to mount. Although some casting materials won't stick to the hair, the chore can cause problems with hair and whiskers. In most instances, you won't be making a full-head cast, but rather individual casts of nose or muzzle and lips, as well as eyes and ear positions. It's important to make the mold as soon as possible after death, as muscle tone deteriorates rapidly and the

eyes will shrink inside the skull fairly quickly. One trick outdoor photographers often use is to insert taxidermist glass eyes over the original eyes to make a dead deer look better for the trophy-pose photos.

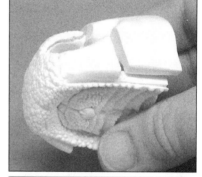

There are two basic casting methods: one that involves a solid mold which must be destroyed to create the positive cast, the other—which is considerably easier—utilizes a flexible mold that can be used several times. Any number of materials can be used to create the negative mold, which is then filled with plaster of paris or urethane to create the positive cast. Premium Latex, Molding Latex, Silicone Rubber and Thixotropic Silicone Rubber are all good choices. Por-A-Mold is an excellent product, but it requires the use of a mold release with it. One of the most popular mold materials with many professional taxidermists is alginate, basically a dental molding material that works extremely well for deep undercuts, allows for super detail and needs no mold separator. The mold must be poured immediately, as it degrades fairly quickly, but it sets in about three minutes.

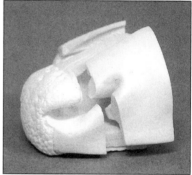

This nose form from Wildlife Artists Supply Company provides extreme detail for reference and comes apart to show interior details as well. (PHOTO COURTESY WASCO)

33

MAKING THE MOLD

Regardless of whether you're making a cast of a muzzle, eye or other body part, the first step is to position the head so the portion to be molded is upright. Use bricks or similar weighty items to prop the head in the desired position and then create a dam around the area to contain the mold material. Cardboard held together with duct tape will serve the purpose. If doing a muzzle, first cut a piece of cardboard to fit around the chin and nose and over the amount of muzzle you wish to mold. Place a piece of clay down in each nostril to prevent the molding material from running down into the nasal passages. If the tongue is protruding, cut it off and make sure the lower jaw is fixed in a realistic position.

Mix the molding material according to the manufacturer's instructions and apply by pouring the material over the muzzle into the contained area. In most instances, several coats of molding will be needed and they must be applied exactly as the material instructions say to assure that they adhere to each other. Except for very small molds, it's wise to add a plaster backing or strengthener to the flexible rubber mold to prevent the plaster used in creating the positive from stretching the thin mold out of shape.

When mixing the molding plaster, you must always add plaster into the water. If you add water to the plaster you'll have lumps at the best, and the material can set up too quickly at the worst. Add the plaster material according to the amount and method described on the package, and stir

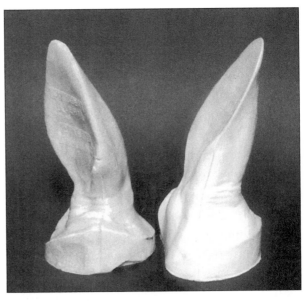

Ear butt details are available from WASCO. (PHOTO COURTESY WASCO

slowly to obtain a creamy, smooth consistency. Normally the plaster has to set for a few minutes and then be stirred again. Once it reaches the proper consistency, apply a thin layer over the rubber mold and allow it to partially

Molded eye details make it easy to locate and mold the eyes and surrounding area. (PHOTO COURTESY WASCO)

set. Apply a thicker layer over the first coat and repeat the process until you build up sufficient coats to provide support before allowing the plaster to set completely. The plaster will heat up at first, and then begin to cool. After it cools down, leave it for about thirty minutes and the finished mold will be ready for removal. Carefully peel the mold away from the area.

With molding materials that deteriorate fairly quickly, such as Alginate, the positive mold must be made almost immediately. Mix the plaster as before, carefully pour it into the cured mold and allow it to set. Occasionally, when removing the mold, you may have to break the plaster backing away to free the rubber mold from deep undercut areas.

Now you have a perfectly detailed positive "sculpture" for future reference, ready to paint, as some taxidermists will, to add even more realistic detail.

4

Measurements

Good visual references are extremely important for realistic deer-head mounting, but proper measurements of the head or body to be mounted are even more critical. Again, these measurements should be done as soon as possible after the animal is killed. Rigor mortis will cause the shape of the body to change; some areas may shrink while other areas expand. The proper measurements are not only necessary for ordering the correct manikin, but also to adjust the manikin in order to fit the skin to it properly. As with visual references, the more measurements you have, the better off you are.

The first step to a quality deer mount is to make notes of any unusual features, such as cowlicks and other unusual hair arrangements, bullet holes and coloration. Also note if antlers are not fairly uniform in shape; you may wish to take photos or make drawings to assure you get them mounted properly. Look at the profile. Is the nose straight or Roman, wide or narrow? Is the neck flared or less full? What regional type does the animal fit? Is it a big-bodied northern whitetail or a Texas deer—more delicate in stature but with exaggerated antler size? What species is it: a whitetail, Coues, blacktail or mule deer? Make as many notes as you can, and take lots of reference photos from different angles.

Before taking the actual measurements, decide where you are going to purchase the manikin, obtain a catalog from the company and make sure to take the measurements according to their instructions. For the most part, the measurements will be consistent, but there may be some minor variations.

MEASURING A FULL, UNSKINNED HEAD

In many instances, particularly with home taxidermy, you'll be using the full, unskinned head as a reference, and it's important to carefully measure the head before it is skinned. Two types of measurements are normally taken—one for commercial or standard purposes, the other for competition work. Even if you're just beginning, the competition measurements will still help a great deal as you form the manikin to suit the skin, and when you purchase eyes, ear liners, and so forth.

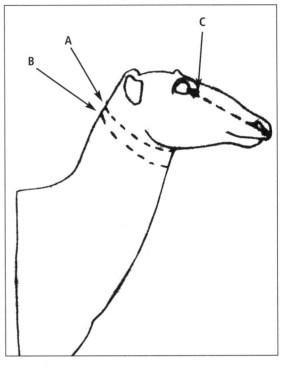

Three basic measurements are necessary for any standard whitetail deer-head mount, and they are best taken with a seamstress or soft-cloth tape measure.

Proper head measurements are extremely important, and you should follow the manufacturer's instructions for the particular manikin you will be using. Shown are the three basic measurements.

The first is from the tip of the nose to the front corner of the eye. The second measurement is the circumference of the neck at the ears. Third, take a measurement three-inches below the ears. I also like to take a fourth measurement, the circumference of the neck approximately halfway down. This additional measurement gives you more detail, especially for full-rut necks.

A competition measurement begins with those same three basics, and then additional measurements are taken, including the distance from the tip of the nose to the corner of the mouth, and from the tip of the nose to the front edge of the bottom lip.

Precise antler placement measurements include one taken three inches from the tip of the nose to the tip of the right antler and another

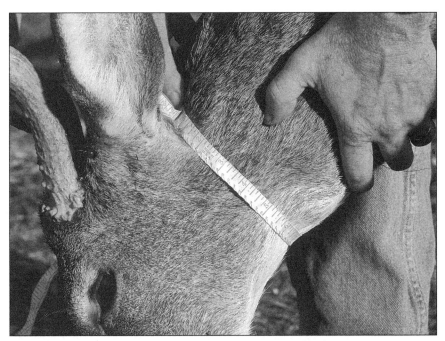

Use a cloth seamstress tape measure and take the first measurements just behind the ears.

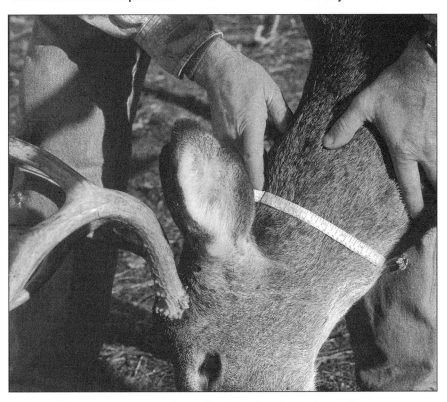

The next measurement is usually taken three inches below the ears.

The third measurement is from the tip of the nose to the front corner of the eye.

taken three inches from the tip of the nose to the tip of the left antler.

Proper eye position also requires precise measurements. First, the size of the eye pupil to determine correct eye size, then the distance across the top of the forehead from the rear corner of each eye to the opposite eye, and finally the same measurement from the front corner of each eye.

These skin-on measurements will give the approximate size used to fit most manikins, although you may also wish to take the same measurements after the animal is caped. You can then send both measurements in ordering the manikin, making sure to indicate which measurements are with the skin on. No manikin will fit a specific deer exactly. Try to acquire the one that comes the closest and be aware that some work will be required in either building up or reducing it to fit the skin. Remember, it is easier to build up small areas than to reduce large areas, so don't make the mistake of buying a somewhat oversized manikin to make an animal appear larger or purchasing a "swelled neck" manikin for a deer head that doesn't have the size to make it look right. Such tactics just won't work.

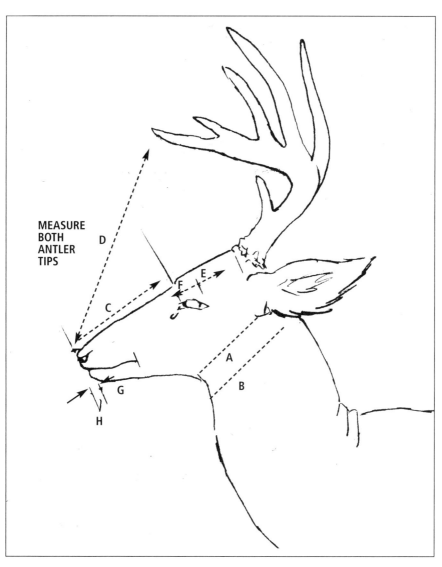

MEASURE
BOTH
ANTLER
TIPS

More detailed measurements can provide a better manikin fit.

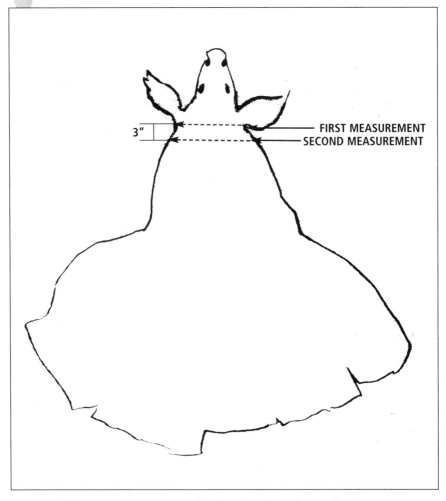

FIRST MEASUREMENT
SECOND MEASUREMENT

3"

Different measurements need to be taken if you have only the cape.

MEASURING A CAPE

If you have a skinned cape to measure, your task is a bit more difficult. A dried hide must first be rehydrated, which means you'll have to mix a solution of one gallon water, one-quarter pound salt and one-eighth teaspoon bactericide. Make enough solution so that the hide is completely submerged and soak it for a couple of hours. Remove the cape and drain it for fifteen minutes, then put it in a plastic bag, but do not tie the bag shut. The cape must be allowed to breathe. Place it in a refrigerator for six to twelve hours. Note: A frozen cape can be treated in the same manner.

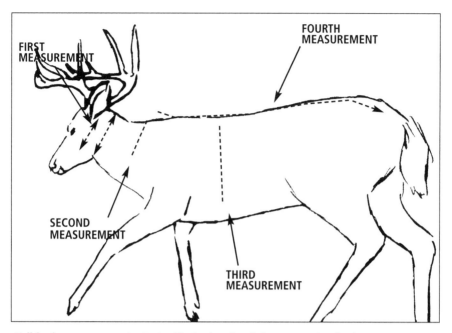

Full-body measurements start with the head and then a couple of other measurements are added.

Remove the cape from the bag and stretch it out for measurements. First, to check its length, grasp the head and brisket and pull firmly. Then grasp the cape directly below both ears and firmly, but slowly, stretch the cape to obtain the width. Watch the brisket and stop stretching when it begins to move. Last of all, take the three basic measurements as for an unskinned head.

FULL BODY

Life-size measurements are a bit more complicated and, if possible, should be taken from an unskinned body. In addition to the basic head measurements, you'll need to measure from the tip of the nose to the base of the tail, as well as the girth of the belly.

Measuring a full body skin is similar to measuring a cape and, once again, measure the head before skinning if possible. Rehydrate the skin and have someone with you to help stretch it. If the head has been skinned, measure as for a cape, stretching for width at the neck, the chest and girth. (The neck is measured by doubling the measurement of a folded skin.) Then measure the length, taking care not to overstretch for this measurement, and the girth at the widest part of the middle belly, but not at the corners of the legs.

Keep all reference materials and measurements in a logbook along with notes on the manikins, eye and ear forms used, and any problems you have in fitting the skin to the manikin. These notes can prove invaluable as you mount future deer heads.

Skinning, Storage, Caping, and Fleshing

Proper skinning, storing, caping, and fleshing are extremely important facets of deer-head mounting. The quality of the steps taken through these procedures will determine the quality of the mount. In some instances, full caping and fleshing may be done during the initial skinning. This is common practice in western hunting camps when the cape may not be transported, tanned, or stored for some time. In most cases, however, the animal is skinned, the cape is stored, sometimes with the head unskinned, or taken to a taxidermist. The head itself may be caped and fleshed at a later date, or completely caped and stored, or caped, fleshed, and then stored. Regardless, fleshing takes quite a bit of time, and one advantage of a do-it-yourself mount is you can tackle these steps as you see fit.

5
Skinning and Storage

T he first step to a quality deer head mount is proper skinning. Hunters can make a number of mistakes in the skinning and field-dressing processes, ruining their chances for a trophy. Granted, an experienced taxidermist can solve many of the problems, but if you're a first-timer, it's wise to make the job as easy as possible.

The first rule is "do not cut the throat." Sounds simple, but it's surprising how many hunters slit the throat of their trophy, and it's a tough fix. In fact, many taxidermists suggest using a neck-only manikin for these mistakes, and then only if the cut is low enough.

Another common mistake is to cut too far up the brisket when field dressing. Again, this can be stitched back together from the inside, but it's a hassle. When field dressing a trophy, cut only up to about five inches behind the front legs.

Finally, don't hang deer by the neck, or tie a rope around the neck to drag a deer out of the woods. Dragging in any form is a serious mistake when you're handling trophy deer. Even if the hair is not abraded completely off, it is usually twisted or bent, creating problems in mounting.

BASIC SKINNING

If possible, hang the deer from a game pole or sturdy tree limb, with a gambrel through the rear hocks. Some skinners like to completely skin the animal, leaving the entire hide intact until they decide to mount the animal, and then cutting the back half of the skin off at that time. This presents more problems in storage, but in most instances the entire animal must be skinned anyway and this is fairly easy to do. You simply cut off the rear portion when you're ready to store or flesh out the skin.

Skinning the cape for mounting can be done in several ways. One method is to skin the entire animal, then cut off the cape portion. In this case, cut around the back legs and then start skinning down the hams.

If you're using this method, cut through the skin around the rear legs just below the hocks before hanging, then cut through the skin at the rear hocks to insert the gambrel. Hoist the carcass until the head and antlers clear the ground and, using a saw, cut off the front legs above the first joint. Then begin skinning at the just-made cuts on the rear legs: Make a cut along the inside of the thigh from the encircling cut down to the opening cut made during field dressing. Peel the skin back over the hams, using a sharp skinning knife to loosen it where necessary. Cut off the tail and then continue peeling the skin down the back, sides and belly, again using a knife as needed. In most instances, the skin will peel off fairly easily with only a little judicious cutting. When you reach the shoulders and neck, peel down to the head and also peel the skin back away from and off the legs. This will take some effort, but you'll end up with a good solid skin that leaves plenty of hide for a good mount. Cut off the head with a bone saw and leave it with the cape for now. Make sure the skin is below the joint of the neck and head, then use a sharp knife to cut through the muscle and tendons down to the bone.

Some people prefer to skin the front half of the deer separately to create the cape, and then they skin the rear half to finish the job. To

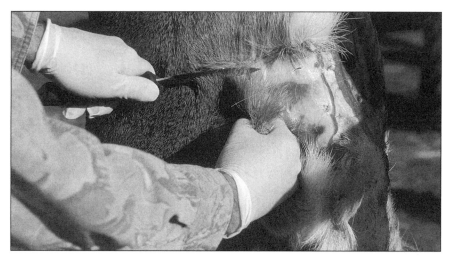

Another method for skinning a trophy for mounting is to cut around the girth well behind the back legs. Then skin out the cape and, finally, the rear half of the hide.

accomplish this, a cut is made completely encircling the chest starting on top of the withers and running under the breastbone, about five to six inches behind the front legs. Then a circle is cut around the front legs just below the elbow joints. In days past, many taxidermists would make a cut along the entire neck, from the withers to just behind the antlers. The cape was opened from the back and skinned down the neck, off the legs and to the head. The head was removed from the body and kept intact with the cape until ready for the fleshing process. During the caping, a "Y" cut was made from the rear cut near the antlers to each antler, then the head skinned out.

Most taxidermists these days utilize a much smaller, less visible cut—basically, about a four-inch extension of the "Y" cut made on top of the head and down the back of the neck during final caping. This requires a great deal less sewing and the stitches are placed in a less visible portion of the mount. The entire neck, including the top portion, is left intact as you skin down to the head, peeling the skin down over the neck as you would pull off a sock. When the joint of the neck and head is reached, the head is cut off in the same manner as before.

SKINNING A FULL-BODY MOUNT

A full-body mount requires a great deal more effort, time, expense and expertise, but it can provide a very interesting and satisfying

Peel and cut the skin down the neck completely to the base of the skull and throat. This does take some work, as the skin is fairly thick.

Once at the base of the skull and throat, use a sharp knife to cut through the muscles and ligaments.

The head can then usually be twisted off, or use an old handsaw to cut it off.

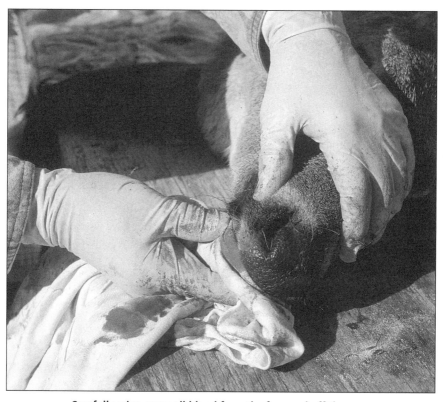

Carefully wipe away all blood from the face and off the cape.

trophy. The carcass is opened on the underside and a cut is made from the tip of the tail, past the anus, the full length of the belly to the brisket between the legs. From this incision, another cut is made on the inside of each leg down to the feet. The skin is peeled away from the legs near the feet and the feet are cut off at the ankle joint.

Once the feet have been removed and the skin pulled down over the rear hocks, a gambrel is inserted and the carcass is hung for further skinning. The skin is peeled away from the entire body and down over the neck to the joint between the neck and head. The head with the full pelt is then cut off and the cape is removed with a small "Y" cut on top of the head during the caping process.

Some hunters will cape out the head at this time as well, although most simply take the cape and head to their taxidermist, letting the professional do the work. Regardless of the method of skinning used for a head mount, the next step is to prepare the cape to protect it until it can be caped and tanned or taken to the taxidermist.

STORAGE

Proper storage of the cape is extremely important. If you have the time and you're already doing the skinning, caping, fleshing and tanning, you may want to skin, cape, flesh and tan as soon after harvesting as possible. Or you can skin, cape and flesh, and then freeze the skin until you get the time to tan it, and if you don't have time to fully flesh the hide, you can simply skin, cape to remove the head, and then freeze.

Don't salt the cape if you can get it to a freezer quickly. Salt causes the flesh to harden, and it can be really tough to get off during the fleshing process. If you're in a remote camp and nowhere near a freezer, however, you should salt the cape to preserve it until you can get to a freezer or have time to tan the hide properly. If that's the case, the skull should be removed, the animal caped and as much flesh taken off as possible before salting. Ordinary stock salt or table salt will serve the purpose, and you should be liberal with the amount you use: about a pound of salt per pound of hide. Make sure you rub the salt into all cracks and crevices, around the eyes and ears and into the nasal cavities. Fold the skin, flesh side to flesh side and then roll it up and place it on an incline with the open end downward so blood and

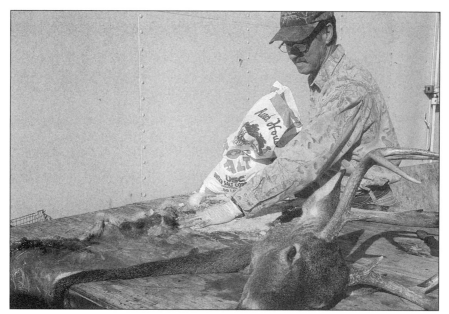

If you can't freeze the cape immediately, it must be well salted. Make sure salt is spread over the entire cape and into ears, eyes, nose, and lips. Then turn the cape flesh to flesh.

other liquids can drain out. You may wish to add salt again the next day, but do not place the hide in a plastic bag or other tight container for transport. It's also best to flesh the hide before you freeze it, as freezing further dehydrates the salted cape.

6
Caping

aping, or removing the skin from the head, may seem daunting to the first-timer, but it's actually fairly easy—although it does take time, and not a little "fiddling" and "tinkering." Plan on taking at least a couple of hours for this chore, especially the first time. Have a good, sturdy worktable at a comfortable height, preferably a table you can sit at.

Caping scares many beginners, but it's not difficult if you take your time and just enjoy the work.

MAKING THE "Y" CUT

At this point, you should have the carcass skinned down to the head with the head still in the cape. As mentioned in the first chapter of this section, most contemporary taxidermists use a small "Y" cut extension for pulling the cape over the skull, creating a "tube" cape instead of an open cape. Begin this cut about two inches below the

Once you have a cape skin with the head attached, make a small "Y" cut at the back of the head.

rear of the antler bases and in the center of the back of the neck, continuing up to each antler base to create a "V" cut. Don't make it too sharp a V, as it will be harder to sew than a flatter, more open V. Do make sure the cut extends up under the burrs of the antlers. Start with the blade down, and then use a sharp pointed knife, blade up, to make the cut. If you examine the back of the head, you'll see an area of long, dark hair that creates a somewhat natural pattern for the cut. Avoid cutting through the hairs, since this will cause sewing and finishing problems later on. One way to keep from cutting through the hairs is to part them and make a light cut as a beginning line to follow. You can then cut from the topside down through the skin, which is the easiest method. After the cuts have been made, grasp the tip of the V-section of skin and, using a small skinning knife, skin out the flap and fold it forward over the forehead.

Make an incision about three to four inches long from the tip of the opened V cut straight down the back of the neck. Again, make sure you don't slice through hairs. Peel the skin back and use a sharp, short skinning knife to release the skin from any muscle tissue. You may have difficulty getting the neck hide completely down and over the skull, since neck hide is fairly thick and tends to "bunch up" when rolled downward without a full back cut. In some instances, you may have to cut away some of the upper neck meat, and then flesh it from

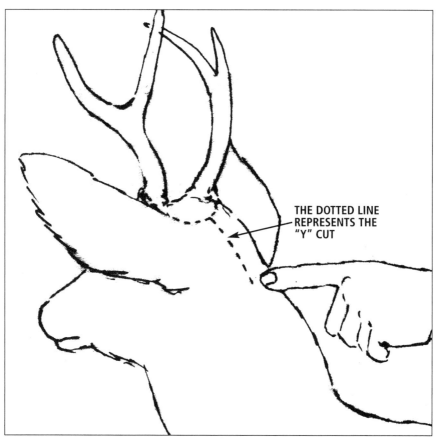

THE DOTTED LINE REPRESENTS THE "Y" CUT

The "Y" cut goes between the two antler bases at the back, then proceeds down the back of the neck for about four to six inches.

the hide as you go. Not having to sew the entire neck later will more than make up for this extra effort up front.

RELEASING THE EARS

As you work the skin around the back of the skull, you will come to the ears. With the skin pulled back, cut through the exposed ear butt as close to the skull as possible. If you cut too far away from the skull, you won't be able to retain ear detail. Cut completely through the ear canal until the ear is loose, being careful not to sever the skin in the front of the ear. Don't worry about the cartilage inside at this point. The ears will be turned inside-out and treated later. Skin up to and cut off each ear as described.

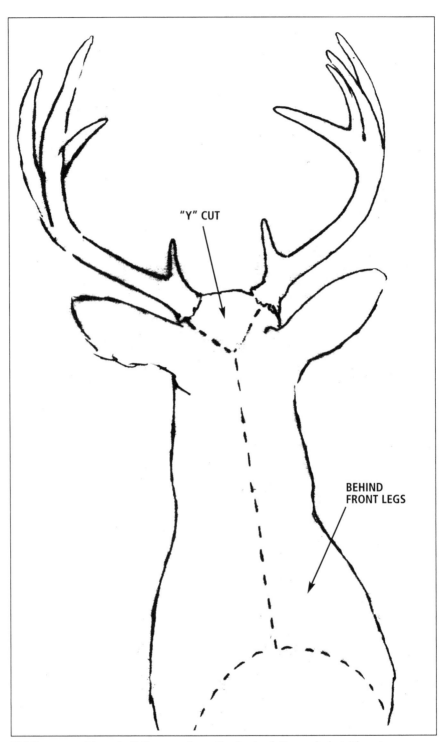

"Y" CUT

BEHIND
FRONT LEGS

Old-timers used to cut all the way down the back of the neck, but it's not necessary.
You can slip the skin off and up over the skull from the underside.

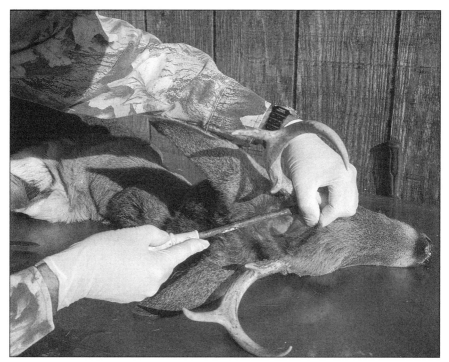

It's extremely important to detach the skin around the base of the antlers, and this is one of the hardest tasks a home taxidermist faces.

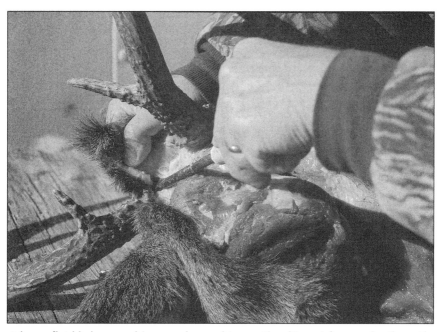

A large, flat-blade screwdriver can be used to pry the skin out from under the antler bases. The author uses a tool with a slightly bent blade, which provides more leverage.

WORKING THE ANTLER BURRS

Here's where some of the hardest work comes in: When you have released both ears, continue skinning until you reach the antler burrs. The skin around them should not be released by cutting, but rather by prying it out and away from under the burrs using a large, flat-bladed screwdriver and following the Y to each antler burr. (My favorite tool for this chore is an old screwdriver with a slightly bent end; it works great.)

Once you have an opening under the antler burr, position the screwdriver with the edge of the blade against the burr and the end of

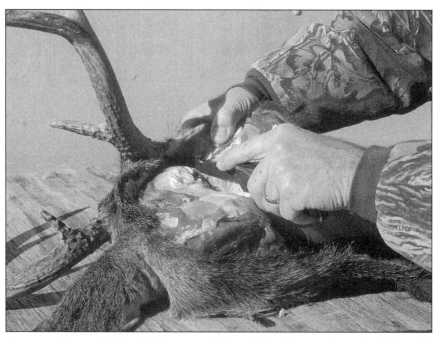

As you work around the antler bases, carefully cut the skin away from the skull on the top of the forehead. When you reach the ear cartilage, cut through it close to the skull.

the blade pointing around the burr. To pry out the skin, tap lightly with a hammer to drive the screwdriver around the burr. As you pry the skin out, use a knife with a short, rounded blade to help release the skin from the skull and flesh. When the hide is completely released from around the antler bases, pull the neck portion of the cape back over the skull cap toward the rearmost front section of the skull, through the Y opening. This will allow you to see what you're doing and continue skinning more easily.

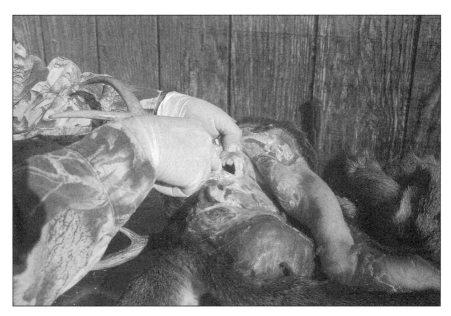

Cut around the eyes very carefully, using your fingers in the eye sockets to guide the knife.

WORKING THE EYES

Keep skinning down to the eyes, pulling the skin over the forehead and down the sides of the skull. Skin the sides of the skull and under the jaw to the eye locations as well. Skinning out the eyes is the trickiest part of the caping chore. Cuts through the skin around the eyes are extremely hard to repair. Take your time and work carefully, making your cuts from the underside of the skin with a small, sharp knife or scalpel. Cut toward the bone and away from

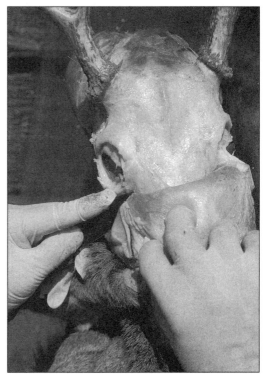

You must also cut and pry the skin gently out of the tear duct in front of the eye.

the eyelid, and hold the skin taut as you work until you reach the eye opening.

Before you begin skinning out the eyelids, place your finger into the eye opening and below the outside of the eyelid. Gently pull the eyelid away from the skull and then use your knife from the underside to cut the skin free from the eye socket. You will be able to feel the knife blade under the skin as you work. Cut completely around the top, bottom and back of the eye, working toward the tear duct. Antlered game, including whitetail deer, have a tear duct directly in front of the eyelid and the skin of the duct is firmly connected to the skull down in a small, depressed channel. Keep the eyelid taut with one hand as you carefully cut and pry the tear duct away from the skull with a scalpel. Skin as close to the bone as possible until you clear the tear duct. Repeat for the opposite eye.

SKINNING LIPS AND NOSE

The lips can be skinned in one of two methods, from the inside or from the outside. Many taxidermists prefer to skin from the inside, merely continuing the skinning process down the face, across the nose and under the jaw, turning the cape downward as they go.

Use short, light strokes down the bridge of the nose and along the

Continue skinning down the nose, sides and under the jaw. Then skin out the lips.

sides of the jaw until you reach the corners of the mouth. Insert your finger into one corner of the mouth and pull the lips away from the skull. Begin cutting around the lips at the corner of the mouth and cut through the cheek muscles about three-quarters of the way from the corners of the mouth. These pieces of meat will be removed during the fleshing process.

Hold the skin taut on the underside of the jaw and skin very closely to the bone, under the jaw and up to the tip of the lower jaw.

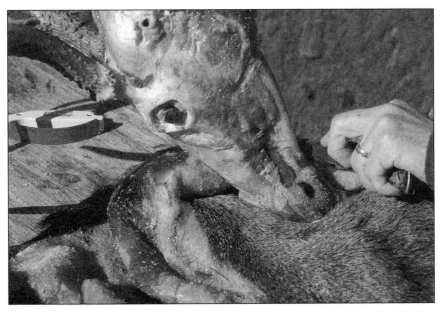

Very carefully skin out the nose, cutting through the cartilage to release the skin from the head.

Cut the lips from the gums as you proceed, holding them out and away and making sure you don't cut through the lower lip when working off the tip at the end of the jaw bone. Continue pulling the upper portion of the cape over the nose and carefully cut away the upper lips until you reach the nose and tip of the upper lip. Skin down the bridge of the nose to the nostrils, peeling the skin back from the bone so you can find the soft nose cartilage with your finger. Carefully cut through the cartilage to the bone, inserting your fingers into the nostrils to help guide the cuts. (Be careful not to cut your fingers!) Continue cutting with small short strokes until you completely free the nose and upper lip.

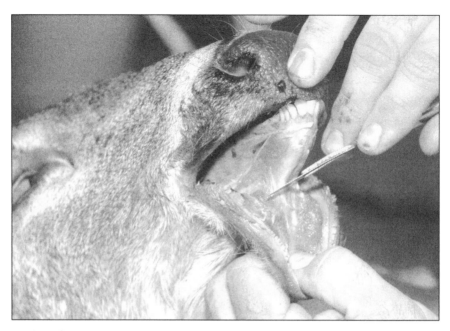

Mark Nash likes to begin the caping chore with the lips and from the outside because he can see what he's doing better. He cuts along the gum line.

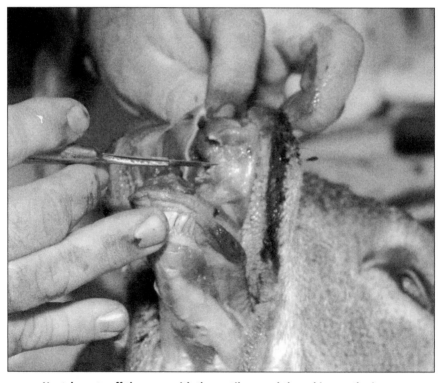

Next, he cuts off the nose with the cartilage and then skins up the jaws.

Skinning the nose and lips from the outside is a somewhat simpler chore that may be more suitable for a first-timer, because it's easier to see what you're doing. After skinning the eyes, position the head with the muzzle facing up and open the mouth. Grasp the nose and pinch it to pull the upper lip tight. Using a scalpel, make an incision along the upper gum line (right at the edge of the palate) and continue the cut to the rear corner of the lips. Be sure to leave about one inch of the lips beyond the hair line attached. Make another incision in the same manner, beginning at the tip of the lower lip and following the lip contour to cut away the lower lip.

To cut away the nose, peel the front of the upper lip that has just been released backward. Then grasp the nose and pull it back and up. Cut through the nose cartilage, following the shape of the bone at the nose, and keep cutting and peeling the skin from around the lips and nose area. Then turn the head around and continue skinning downward along the bridge of the nose and jaws to meet the cuts made in releasing the lips and nose.

At this time the cape should be completely free of the skull.

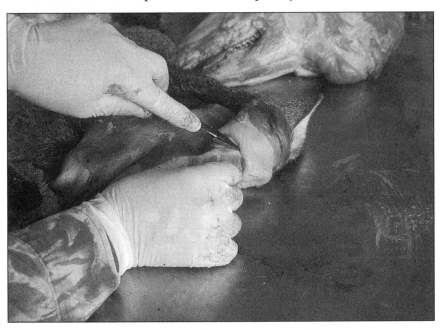

In "turning" the ears, the cartilage side of the ears is turned wrong-side out. Begin with a round-point skinning knife to cut the skin back away from the ears butts.

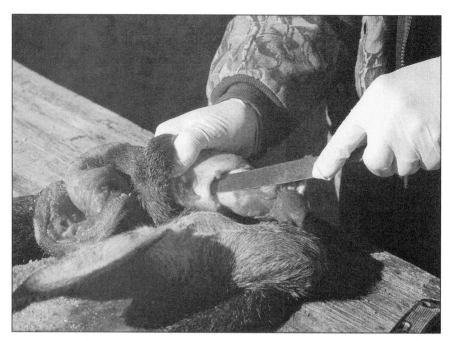

Use the flat, rounded blade of an unsharpened table knife to work in and around the ears to turn them, or buy yourself a special ear-turning tool.

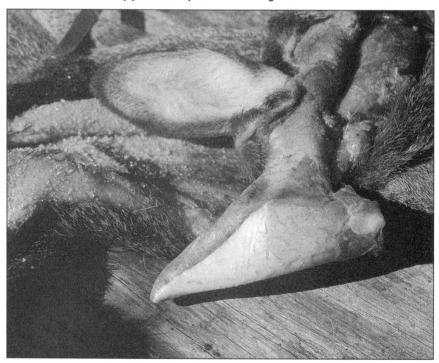

The resulting "turned" ear.

The lips must be split to allow for proper storage or tanning.

REMOVING THE ANTLER PLATE

At this point, remove the antler plate by making a cut directly behind the eyes and vertically down through the skull using a hacksaw, fine-toothed handsaw or bone saw. Continue the cut until it reaches past the eyes, then make a sec-ond cut from the top of the head to meet the first, until the antler plate is freed. Scoop out any brain matter and scrape off any flesh. To loosen any flesh that remains, bring a solution of Sal Soda to a boil, place the skull plate into the solution and then simmer the skull for about half an hour. Use a skinning knife to scrape away any remaining matter, leav-ing yourself with a clean antler plate that will not attract insects.

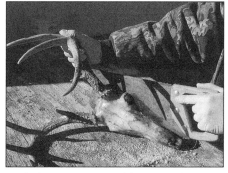

With the cape removed from the skull, the antlers are cut away.

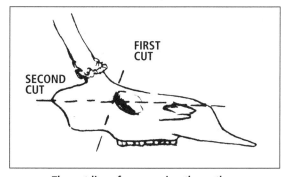

The cut lines for removing the antlers.

7
Fleshing

Proper fleshing is the next important step, and it can be quite time consuming, especially for a first-timer. "I have had several people say they want to learn how to mount a deer head, but usually give up halfway through the fleshing process," said taxidermist Mark Nash. "You can count on at least five to six hours for your first fleshing job."

FLESHING EARS

Turn the ears wrong side out by pushing the ear butt outward and peeling the ear skin back. Use a scalpel to release the ear butt and then to cut carefully between the outside ear covering and the cartilage of the ear butt. This cartilage is firmly attached to the front of the ear but not

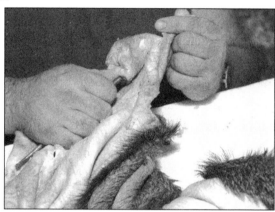

Proper fleshing of the cape is vital. The ears may require additional turning to bring the edges out fully, and if the ears haven't been turned, this is the time to do so. Use a scalpel to make these last few cuts. (Most taxidermists like to leave the cartilage attached until later.)

to the back. Once you have the ear about halfway skinned, use a round-edged table knife, a thin, flat-pointed wooden stick, or a large, flat-bladed screwdriver with rounded corners to work between the skin on the back and the cartilage in the ear. Go very carefully and avoid pushing the tool through the thin skin around the edge of the ear. A special tool called an ear-turner makes this chore easier and quicker, and helps prevent tearing the delicate skin.

Regardless of the tool used, continue working until you can turn the ear completely inside out, leaving the cartilage attached to the front ear skin and using a scalpel to remove all meat and muscle from the ear butt. Some taxidermists like to remove the cartilage liner at this time, before pickling and/or tanning. Others prefer to wait until after those steps, when the skin is tougher and it's somewhat easier to keep it from tearing. Also, if using the bonded-ear method, the cartilage is left intact to the ear. If using a commercial ear liner, the cartilage will have to be removed at a later time.

FLESHING THE EYES

Next comes the tricky part. The flesh around the eyes and nose must be removed from the skin. Mark Nash uses a pair of wooden fleshing instruments to do this chore: One is a cone-shaped piece with a rounded ball shape on the narrow end—a handy device for general fleshing around the eyes. The skin is pulled over the rounded ball,

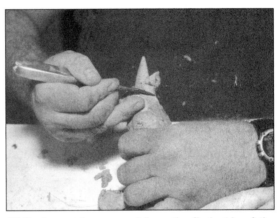

All flesh must be removed from the flesh side of the skin around the eyes, and this is delicate work. A wooden fleshing instrument shaped with a small rounded end can be placed in the eye from the hair side to stretch the skin taut for easier fleshing.

flesh side up. A sharp scalpel is then used to very carefully cut away all flesh and to slightly thin the skin around the eyes and eyelids. Incidentally, an ordinary wooden colander food masher can be used for these chores. The other tool is shaped like a small horn, with a smooth, sharp but rounded end. A special narrow, pointed but round-ended fleshing board can also be made for the purpose.

The tear duct inside the back of both bottom and top eyelids must also be opened, and there is a fairly thick "gristle" along each side of the tear duct that must be very carefully removed. By holding the eyelid with your finger on the outside, you'll be able to feel the tiny ridge where the tear duct is located. Very carefully make a shallow

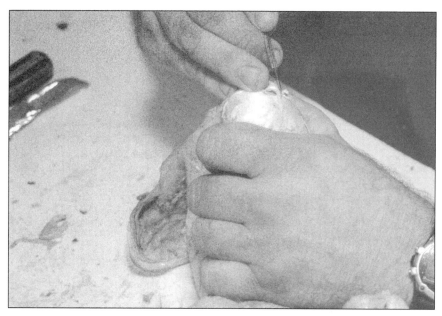

The thick gristle must be removed from the tear-duct area.

incision following this ridge on the inside of the eyelid and gently scrape out the tiny yellow "fat" globules you'll see there. If you fail to do this, the inside of these glands will gradually dry and shrink causing the eyes to have an unrealistic appearance, weeks or months after the mounting has been finished.

With your scalpel, flesh all around the inner face, around the eyes and to at least two to three inches past the eyes in all directions. The inner eye membrane

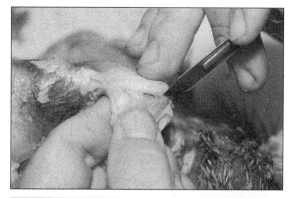

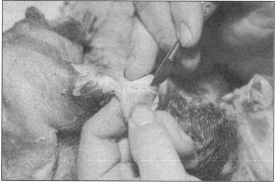

These two images show how the tear ducts on the underside of each eyelid must be opened and the tiny yellow globules scraped away.

71

should also be shortened somewhat, but make sure you leave at least 3/8- to 1/2-inch for proper tucking of the membrane during the eye-set procedure.

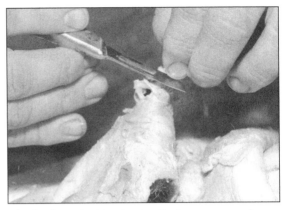

FLESHING THE NOSE

The next step is to flesh the nose, and the best method is to work

It's also important to shorten the inner eye membrane somewhat, but leave at least 3/8- to 1/2-inch for tucking.

with a cone-shaped wooden object placed through the nostril from the outside, pulling the nostril tight over the cone. You can then use a

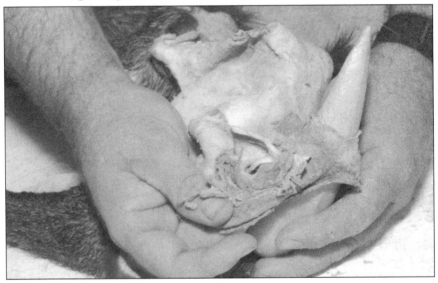

The nose is fleshed in the same manner. Again, a form is pushed through the nostril to hold the skin taut and allow for careful fleshing with a scalpel. Cut off excess material.

scalpel to remove all the flesh and, finally, cut back and remove the cartilage, leaving only the skin in the nostril openings. You must flesh down until you can see the backs of the individual hair follicles of the nose, which will look like dark spots. Do not flesh any deeper once you find the dark spots representing individual hair follicles, or you risk cutting these hairs loose.

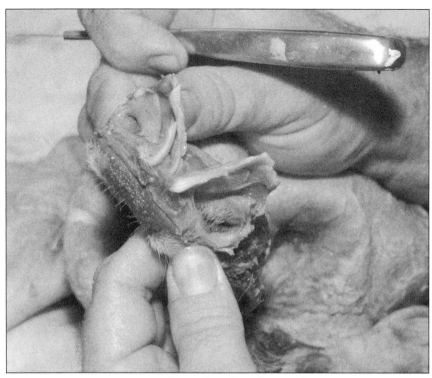

Remove the cartilage from the nostrils.

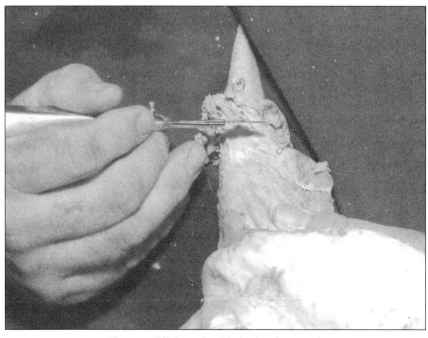

The nostril linings should also be shortened.

FLESHING THE LIPS

The lips must be split to allow for proper hide preservation. This consists of simply separating the outer and inner lip skin and cutting away the inner portion, leaving only the outer skin for the lip-tucking procedure. Like the eye and nose work, this is a delicate task and it does take some time. Go very carefully and try not to make any slips, since lip cuts can be extremely tough to repair. Make sure your workplace

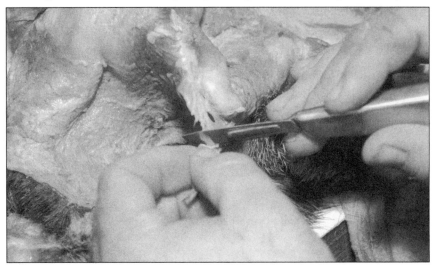

The lips require quite a bit of work. They must be split and all excess flesh and membrane must be removed in order for the tanning agents to work.

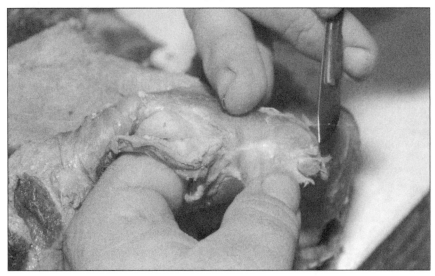

Splitting the lips involves separating the inner and outer portions of the lips and cutting away the inner lining.

has good light so you can see well, and that your scalpel is sharp.

CAPE FLESHING

With the delicate parts finished, it's time for the overall fleshing of the cape. Mark Nash uses a big bowie knife for removing the bulk of the flesh

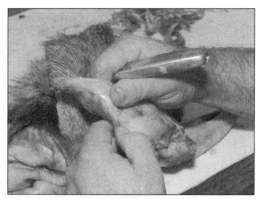

This leaves only the outer lip "skin."

from his capes, and any sharp, long-bladed knife will get the job done. But a real fleshing knife can make the chore easy and quick. The hide should be placed over a fleshing beam, and a bench or floor model, as illustrated in the chapter on tools, will serve the purpose. Try to make sure all flesh is completely removed. Although any flesh left can be taken off during the thinning procedure, after

the pickle bath, it's best to remove as much as possible in this first fleshing operation. Also note, if you're using a dry one-day tan, all the flesh must be removed at this time.

Make sure to turn both the inner and outer skin completely out to the edges. The remainder of the cape should then be well fleshed. Mark Nash simply uses a big hunting knife for the task.

Pickling, Thinning, and Tanning

Tanning is the most important step of preserving the hide or cape. Basically, it involves first removing the hypodermis and adipose, that is, the underlying layers of membrane and fat (fleshing). Then the skin must be stabilized and preserved to keep the collagen proteins that make up the skin cells from putrefying. The tanning process modifies the chemical structure of the proteins, creating a stable, hair-on skin that will not rot, fall apart or have an odor.

In the past, various traditional dry-preservative methods were used, and if you examine many older mounts, you'll notice hair slipping, skin curling, shrinkage, and other problems. Today's easy-to-use, consistent and quality tanning agents are responsible for major advances in taxidermy. Some taxidermists prefer to send the cape out to a commercial tanner, and in the past that was fairly common. However, tanning is a very simple process that can be done in your own shop, basement or garage. It does require attention to detail and some work, but home tanning also eliminates the delay in waiting for the cape to be returned, which could take weeks.

Several different methods may be used—some traditional, others that utilize modern materials and tactics. If you are using a kit, your main concern is following the instructions for the materials supplied with care. If not, your first consideration is to determine the tanning agent you want to use (See Section II, Chapter 2, Materials). In most instances, the tanning agent instructions will also indicate what additional steps are necessary with that particular material, such as salting and/or pickling.

8
Pickling and Thinning

In general, pickling and salting are the first steps in cape preservation. Immediately after the pre-fleshing steps and before the pickling process, the hide must be washed thoroughly in cold water with a detergent (Era seems to do a good job) and a bactericide. If there is excess blood on the hide, a blood remover may also be needed. The skin should then be rinsed thoroughly in cold water and placed in a tumbler or clothes washer on the spin cycle to eliminate some of the water. (Do not wring or twist the skin.) It's a good idea to take these steps immediately after skinning if possible, and then repeat after the initial fleshing.

Examine the skin and make sure all flesh and membranes are removed. Then hang the skin up for about thirty minutes to allow it to drain.

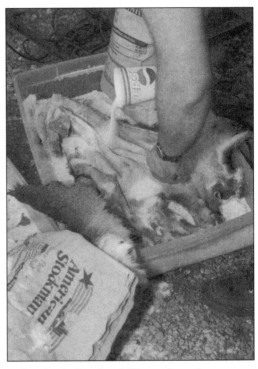

Before beginning the pickling and tanning processes, it's a good idea to wash the cape in cold water with detergent and a bactericide added, to remove blood and dirt. Allow the cape to drain for approximately thirty minutes, and then begin the preserving process by salting the skin. Work the salt well into all flesh surfaces and around the eyes, ears, lips, and nostrils.

Fold the skin, flesh-to-flesh, and roll it up. Then put it in a cool place with the open end down so it will drain.

SALTING

The age-old method of salting hides to "set the hair" and begin the preserving process comes next. Spread the skin out and rub salt into the flesh-side surface. Use plenty of salt and make sure all areas are covered, including in and around the ear butts, the eyes and the lips, rubbing or pressing the salt into the skin with your fingers. You can use non-iodized table salt, but stock salt is the most economical.

Reapply the salt in twenty-four hours.

Once the skin is well salted, fold it in half lengthwise, flesh-to-flesh, and then roll it up loosely and put it in a cool place with the open end down to allow for drainage. Leave the skin for at least twenty-four hours, reapply the salt and allow it to sit for another twenty-four hours. The skin is now ready for pickling or tanning, depending on the method used, and either way, it's best to do this immediately.

PICKLING FORMULAS

Check to determine if the tanning agent you are using requires pickling. (Some don't.) If it's needed, Bruce Rittel of Rittel's Tanning Supplies suggests leaving the skins in the pickle for three days, then removing, draining, shaving, washing and rinsing then, and returning them to the pickle for another twelve to twenty-four hours.

Following are standard formulas commonly used throughout the tanning industry. Although these are intended for "static" use, such as "Garbage Can Pickling," they should receive mild agitation. In fact, all pickles should be stirred at least once or twice daily and the pH checked as well. The temperature should be kept at 65 to 80 degrees F.

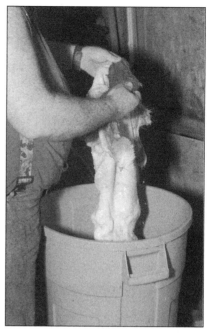

The most common kind of pickling is the "garbage barrel" method, which refers to soaking the cape or capes in a garbage barrel with the pickling solution. The capes should be stirred regularly.

PICKLING WITH SULFURIC ACID

- 1 fluid ounce sulfuric acid
- 1 pound salt
- 1 gallon water
- Dissolve the salt in the water and then slowly pour the acid into the water, stirring the mixture throughout the process.

PICKLING WITH OXALIC ACID

- 2 ounces oxalic acid crystals
- 1/4 pound salt
- 1 gallon water
- Heat a quart of water and dissolve the acid crystals and salt in the warm liquid. Then pour in three more quarts of water. Allow to cool before using.

PICKLING WITH FORMIC ACIC

- 1.1 ounce (by weight) 85% formic acid
- 1 pound salt
- 1 gallon water
- Dissolve the salt in the water and then slowly pour the acid in, stirring the mixture as the acid is poured.

PICKLING WITH ACETIC ACID

- 2 ounces acetic acid (56%)
- 1 pound salt
- 1 gallon water
- Dissolve the salt in the water and then slowly pour the acid into the water, stirring the mixture as the acid is poured.

PICKLING WITH CITRIC ACID

- 3 ounces citric acid
- 1 pound salt
- 1 gallon water
- Dissolve the salt in the water and then slowly pour in the acid, stirring the mixture throughout the process.

PICKLING WITH WHITE VINEGAR

- 2 quarts white vinegar
- 2 quarts water
- 1 pound salt
- Stir all together until salt is completely dissolved.

PICKLING WITH SODIUM BISULFATE

- 4 ounces sodium bisulfate
- 1 pound salt
- 1 gallon water
- Dissolve the salt and sodium bisulfate in the water.

PICKLING WITH ALUM

- 12.8 ounces aluminum sulfate
- Or 12.8 ounces ammonium aluminum sulfate
- Or 12.8 ounces potassium aluminum sulfate

- 1 pound salt
- 1 gallon water
- Dissolve the salt and sulfate in the water.

PICKLING WITH MURIATIC ACID

- 1 ounce muriatic acid
- 1 pound salt
- 1 gallon water
- Dissolve the salt in the water, then stir in the muriatic acid.

Important Safety Notes: Many of the acids are quite dangerous, so handle all chemicals very carefully and always wear eye and face protection, long-sleeved shirts, rubber gloves and a rubber apron. Always pour the acid into the water; never pour the water into the acid. Store chemicals in a safe place and make sure your storage area and workplace have adequate ventilation.

USING SAFTEE-ACID

Rittel's Saftee-Acid is, as its name implies, one of the safest acids available today. It provides a wide range of acidity with none of the disadvantages of sulfuric, formic, acetic, oxalic and other commonly used acids. It is non-poisonous, practically odorless–which means no caustic fumes. It also has no dilution heat and is non-evaporative, making it an excellent choice for pickling as well as adjusting pH levels. What's more, since it is non-hazardous, it is safe to ship anywhere, and because of its low dosage, it's a money saver.

Always weigh your skins before preparing a pickling formula and use two quarts of water for every one pound of wet-drained skin weight. For every one gallon of pickle needed, use one gallon of water, one pound of non-iodized salt and one-half fluid ounce of Rittel's Saftee-Acid SA-200. This ought to give you a pH level of about 1.0, and as long as you hold the pickle below a 2.0 (normally it varies between 1.1 and 1.5), you should have no problems. It usually remains very stable, but don't forget to check the pH level daily.

Leave the cape in the pickle for three days, until it is thoroughly pickled. Then remove it, wash it in cold water and allow it to drain for about thirty minutes. Shave or thin the skin, then return it to the pickle for another twelve to twenty-four hours. If you maintain the pH on a daily basis, you can leave the cape in the pickle for quite some time, until you are ready to neutralize and tan the skin.

If the cape has been flint dried, it should be rehydrated before pickling in a solution of one pound salt to each five gallons of water and a couple of ounces of Dawn dish soap or Era washing detergent. Rinse in cold water to remove all soap and salt and allow to drain for about thirty minutes.

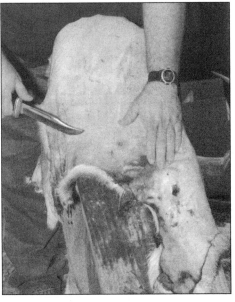

Remember, if you're using a kit that comes with pickling solution, follow the manufacturer's instructions.

THINNING

Now it's time to thin, or shave, the back side of the skin so it will take the tan evenly and be more malleable when you work it onto the form. The easiest way to thin hide is with a power circular-blade

The next step is to thin the entire cape so the tan will take evenly. This can be done over a fleshing beam with a fleshing knife, or using a wire wheel in a portable electric drill.

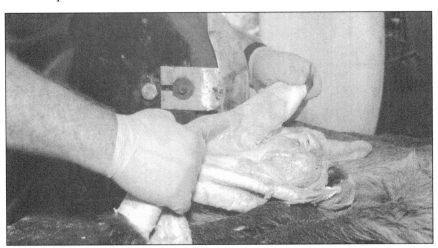

A fleshing wheel makes the chore much easier and the results more uniform.

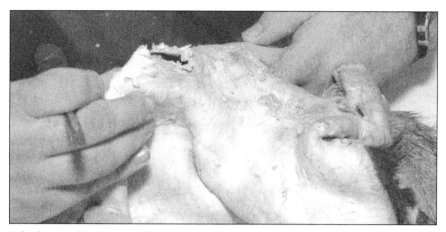

Check around the eyes, ears, lips, and nose and repeat any thinning that may be necessary.

fleshing or shaving machine. You can also use a wire wheel in a portable electric drill, as long as you make sure you don't hold it in one spot too long and "burn" a hole in the cape. A farrier's rasp can also be used. For both of the latter two methods, you'll need to position the cape over a fleshing beam.

Check around the eyes and lips and make sure they are well fleshed and thinned. Mark Nash also recommends thinning the edges of the cape where any sewing must be done, as it makes the stitching much easier. Then return the thinned skin to the pickle bath for the amount of time indicated.

NEUTRALIZING

Before tanning, the acid from the pickling bath must be neutralized by adding one ounce of sodium bicarbonate (baking soda) to each gallon of water. Mark suggests adding some Era washing detergent to the water as well. Wash the cape thoroughly to remove all the pickling solution and then rinse it completely in cold water. The cape is now ready to be tanned or

Before tanning, neutralize the pickling acid by washing the cape in a solution of cool water and sodium bicarbonate, with just a bit of washing detergent added.

frozen and stored until you have time to do the tanning.

9
Tanning

One of the biggest problems in old-time mounts was poor tanning of the cape. Often it was merely preserved with Borax. These days you can choose from a number of tanning agents, as described in Section I, Chapter 2, and methods that include wet, oil-based and dry tans. (Again, if using a kit, follow the instructions that come with it.)

WET TANS

One of the simplest and most effective wet tans is Rittel's EZ-100. A powdered Syntan tanning and synthetically manufactured Sulphonic Acid agent, it eliminates environmental and personal handling problems. It contains no metallic components, but produces a stretchy, durable cape with negligible shrinkage, and a long life. It also costs less than many other tanning agents.

These days any number of excellent tanning agents is available for mounting deer heads. The choice depends on personal preference. For wet tans, the skins are soaked in a liquid solution.

After the pickling and neutralizing process, drain the skin for about an hour. Wet tanning agents are very sensitive to pH (for example, EZ-100 tans at a pH level of 4.0), so always check it before placing the cape into the solution and then check again thirty minutes later. Add very small amounts of baking soda if the pH is high or small amounts of citric acid or white vinegar if the pH is low.

When mixing the tanning solution, add the EZ-100 first and stir until it dissolves, then add the salt. If tanning more than one cape at a time, add them all simultaneously, since EZ-100 is a fast tanner and the first cape may deplete the solution before the last cape is placed in the tan.

EZ-TANNING FORMULA (BASED ON WET-DRAINED WEIGHT)

After neutralizing the cape and allowing it to drain for one hour, weigh it to determine the wet-drained weight and use this weight to calculate the amount of tanning solution needed. It is the most accurate and least wasteful method. For every one pound of drained weight, mix:

- 2 quarts of water
- 1/2 ounce of EZ-100 (4-1/2 level teaspoons = 1/2 oz.)
- 4 ounces of salt

EZ-TANNING FORMULA (BASED ON WATER VOLUME)

After neutralizing the cape and letting it drain for one hour, mix enough solution to completely cover the cape, since this formula is based on the amount of water it takes to cover the cape. For every one gallon of water needed, mix:

- 1 gallon water
- 1 ounce of EZ-100 (3 level tablespoons = 1 oz.)
- 8 ounces of salt

It is extremely important not to overcrowd the capes if you're tanning more than one at a time, and note that both these solutions must be kept at a comfortable room temperature between 65 and 75 degrees F. Leave the cape or capes in the tanning solution for sixteen to twenty hours. Almost all capes will tan thoroughly within twenty-four hours, and you should never overtan. After twenty-four hours, pull the cape from the tanning solution, rinse and allow it to drain for no more than twenty minutes. If you have a dry sawdust tumbler, you can tumble the cape for about five minutes to remove the surface moisture only and then gently blow away the sawdust with an air gun.

After the cape has dried for twenty minutes and has reached room temperature, lay it out flat and apply a hot oil/water mixture to the flesh side using a paint brush. (Rittel's ProPlus Oil mixed with two parts hot tap water is excellent for this purpose.) Apply the oil mixture while it is still hot, working carefully along the edges and around holes. When the cape is fully oiled, fold it flesh to flesh and lay it aside in a warm area to sweat in the oil for four to six hours. Maximum absorption of the oil will take place during this sweating period.

After sweating, the skin can be briefly tumbled to damp dry or toweled to damp dry and then mounted, or frozen to be thawed and mounted later. Use a degreaser to clean up any oil splashed on the hair.

FORMIC ACID

Formic acid is a traditional taxidermy tan that involves using the same basic formula and tactics as for pickling. You maintain the pH between 2.2 and 2.5 and keep the tan at a temperature of around 70 degrees F.

After salting and rehydration, place the cape in the solution and leave it overnight, making sure to agitate often so that the solution reaches into the ears and all parts of the hide. Next day, drain, reflesh or thin as needed, place the cape back in the pickle solution and agitate it frequently. Take it out the following day, drain it and once again reflesh or thin as needed. Examine the areas around the eyes and thin there as well, and remove the ear cartilage. Return the cape to the pickle bath and leave for another day or two. It should be completely white and tanned in three to four days.

Remove it, neutralize it and wash it thoroughly using a moth-proofing bath of Edolan-U and following the manufacturer's instructions.

The final step is oiling the cape to prevent shrinkage and increase its flexibility for during mounting. A sulfinated tanning oil mixed half and half with hot tap water should be liberally brushed over the flesh side. The oil should be allowed to soak in for a couple of hours, but do not let it get on the hair.

OIL TANS

Oil tans are some of the easiest to use. Once the cape has been properly pickled, neutralized and washed, the hide is laid out flat on a smooth surface and an oil tan, such as Syn Oil, is rubbed onto the flesh side. The hide is folded flesh to flesh and the oil is allowed to work for the amount of time indicated by the manufacturer's instructions.

Rinehart's Tanning Cream is used in much the same manner. Before tanning, it is suggested the cape be washed in a moth-proofing solution, such as 1-10 Edolan-U solution. Basically the same moth-proofing chemical used to protect wool clothing, it helps prevent insect infestation. Borax, six ounces by volume to five gallons of water. should also be used along with the mothproofing. Agitate vigorously, then drain for an hour, or put it in an automatic washer on spin cycle.

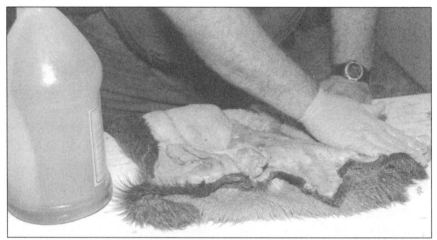

Oil tans are extremely easy to use. They are rubbed into the flesh side of the hide. Make sure the tanning agent is rubbed in well in all places such as around eyes, ears, nose and lips.

Spread the cape out, hair side down, and brush a liberal coat of the tanning cream over the entire flesh side, making sure to cover all cracks and crevices, and the openings in and around ears, nose and eyes. Do not fold the cape, as the cream must be allowed to penetrate into the skin. After it has penetrated, the skin will be ready for mounting and can be mounted the same day.

A cream-tanned cape that's left overnight for maximum penetration must be covered with plastic to prevent excess drying. If it seems to be somewhat dry, sponge on water to soften. If you plan on storing your cream-tanned cape for over twenty-four hours, place it in a plastic bag and refrigerate. If the cape is going to be stored for more than forty-eight hours, it should be placed in a plastic bag and frozen. Just before mounting, spray a heavy coat of 1-10 Edolan-U on the skin, allow it to penetrate and then start your mount.

The hide is then folded flesh-to-flesh and allowed to work for the amount of time as directed by the manufacturer.

SECTION V

Form Preparation

10

Form Modeling

W hile the cape is pickling and/or tanning is a good time to prep the form to receive it. If you have measured correctly, the form should fit fairly well. However, some shaping will almost always be required.

First, set up a means of holding the form while you work on it. You can purchase a mounting stand, although they're a bit costly for the first-timer or occasional hobbyist. If you're fairly proficient as a welder, you can also make up your own mounting stand.. Or you can try the R.A.M. system used in the marine industry to mount electronics and fishing rod holders on boats. It's also a great tool for holding head forms. The R.A.M. system, which consists of a ball with a clamp, can be attached to a bench or other solid surface. Buy a two-foot section of threaded two-inch steel pipe and thread a metal flange on the end. Fasten the flange to the back of the form board with wood screws or lag bolts. The pipe can then be clamped in a sturdy vise to hold the form for working. If you want an even simpler method, screw a two-inch by four-inch by six-inch block to the back and clamp the block in the vise.

Some taxidermists attach the wall hanging bracket to the wooden backing of the head form at this time, which is easier than waiting until after the head has been mounted. Any number of commercial hangers can be used, as long as they are sturdy enough to hold the weight. You can also simply bore a shallow hole in the back of the panel and screw a small angle iron to the top edge to create a hanger.

The hanger should be placed as close to the top edge as possible to prevent the mount from turning sideways on the wall from the weight of the antlers. The reason some taxidermists prefer to fasten the hanger after the head is mounted is that it allows for a more precise location, enabling them to make sure the head will hang straight. This is especially critical with turned heads, when one side may be heavier than the other.

FORM MODELING

With the form held securely, the next step is to roughen its entire surface to remove any mold release and help the hide paste work better as you glue the cape to the form. Roughing can be done with a rasp/file or with 60 grit sandpaper. Or you can buy special tools called a Stout Ruffers, available in several sizes. You can use one of the larger models for general roughing and a narrower one for getting under the jaw and into other tight places. Take your time when doing this and make sure you smooth all roughened surfaces. If there is a mold release line, make sure this is sanded or rasped off.

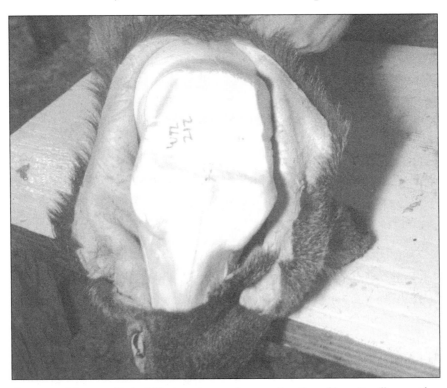

You may wish to try-fit the hide to get a rough approximation of how it will cover the form. First, see if the hide fits around the neck.

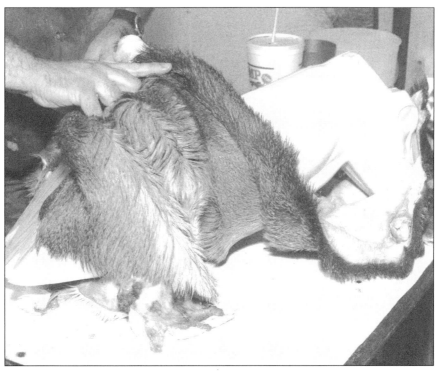

Then check the brisket area to make sure the hide comes down and covers the backboard.

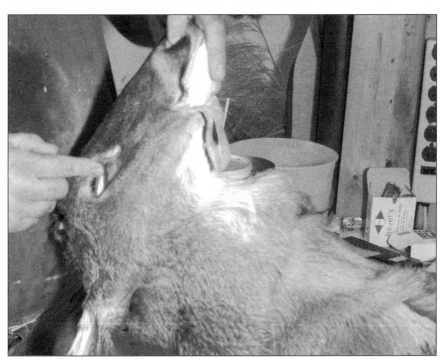

Finally, check the eye and ear locations.

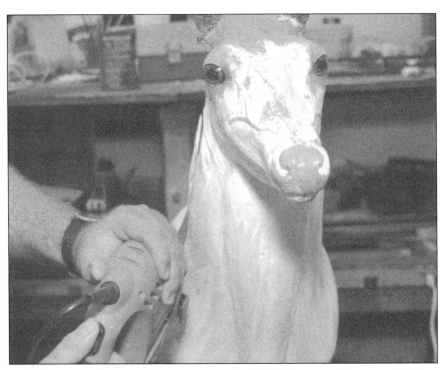

If the form is too large, you can trim some material. If it's too small, you can build up with clay, but it's best to have a form that fits the cape.

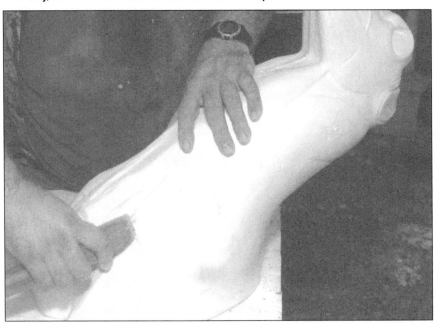

The form must be roughed up to assure the form glue will adhere. A rasp, rough sandpaper, or a taxidermist's Stout Ruffer can be used to roughen the surface. This process is not a substitute for modeling.

The Stout Ruffer is available in several sizes, including smaller tools to work under the chin and in tight spots.

It's important to remove all mold lines or "flashings." You may also wish to emphasize certain muscles, but make sure you have good references before you attempt it.

Using a modeling tool or a tiny power rotary tool such as a Dremel, deepen the nostrils if needed. In most instances, the nasal openings will be fairly shallow to allow the form to release. Do not reshape the outside; open up the interior only, as this will be needed to properly shape the nasal passage and to hold the clay that helps keep the nostril skin in place. You should also make a fairly deep cut in the center of the nostrils with the modeling tool, following the

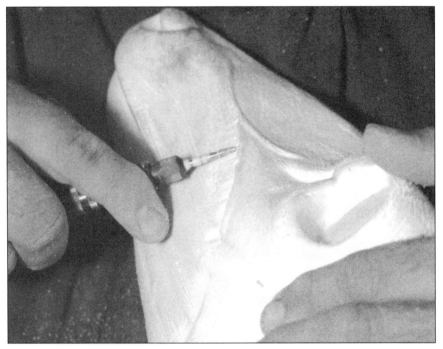

If you're really interested in detailing, a Dremel tool and small grinder bit can be used to deepen the veining on the nose.

contour of the nasal opening. This will also help hold the tucked nostril skin in place. Mark Nash recommends using a whitetail nose reference to assure the modeling is correct. He fastens it in place over the form nose and models to copy it.

The tear duct in the eye will need to be shaped, which involves making a cut with a modeling tool or scalpel and following the tear duct on the form. The cut should begin about 3/8-inch from the front corner of the eye and following the form modeling for about 3/4-inch.

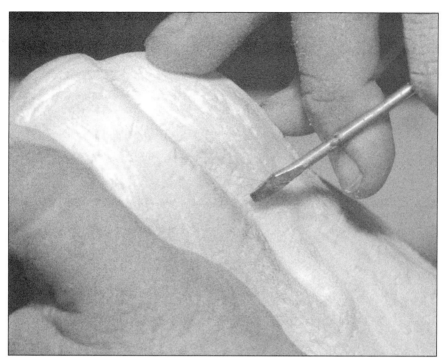

The form's mouth or lip line should be cut or deepened to receive the lips as they are tucked in place. A small screwdriver is excellent for this job, or you can use a modeling tool.

Check the eye or eye system being used. In some cases, you may have to model the eye socket.

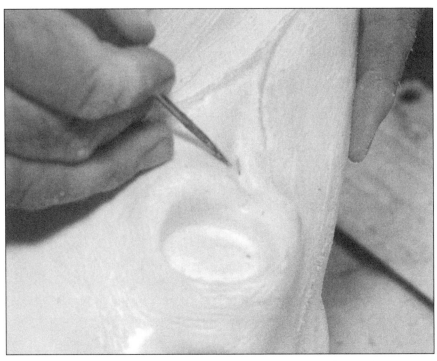

Deepen the tear duct with a small screwdriver or modeling tool.

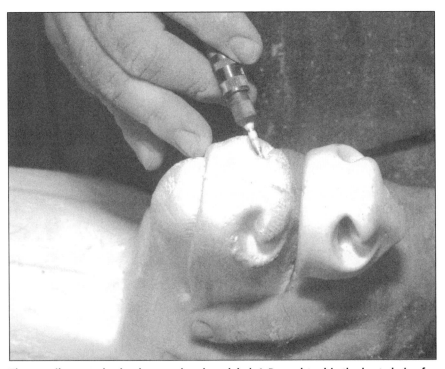

The nostrils must also be deepened and modeled. A Dremel tool is the best choice for this chore.

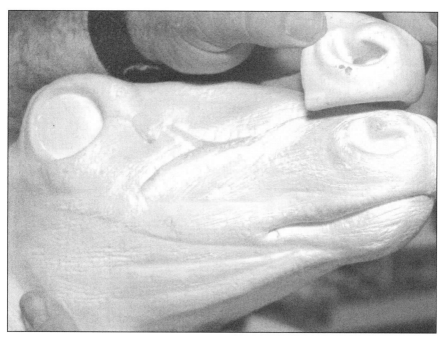

A good reference form is invaluable for working around the muzzle. Nash attaches the reference "mask" to the form with a nail for precise modeling.

Also, check the eye or eye system being used. In many instances, you'll need to do some carving of the sockets to get the eyes or eye system to fit properly.

The lip slot should be opened using the modeling tool or a 1/8-inch rotary rasp. Before making this cut, use a marking pencil to draw the line following the joining of the lips and where you want to cut. Then make the cut starting at one corner of the mouth and proceeding around to the opposite corner.

Mark Nash, who likes to deepen the veining on the face of the form, uses a rotary tool with a small rasp to cut back the material around the veining. This makes the facial veining more pronounced. Some taxidermists also like to use a large nail to punch holes in the ear butt area, which helps to anchor whatever material they're using to attach the ear butts.

ANTLER ATTACHMENT

Proper positioning and attachment of the antlers is vital, and your chore will be much easier if you have taken the correct measurements from the unskinned deer head. Different forms have different antler-mounting methods, and it's important to follow the manufacturer's instructions for the forms you use. In all cases, the first step is to mark the centerline of the skullcap—a slight but sharp rise of the skull. The form should have a corresponding ridge, and you should mark the center of this as well.

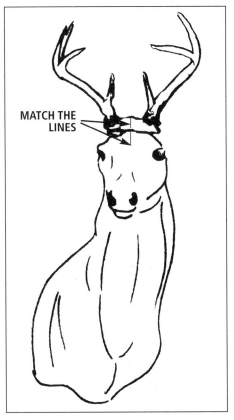

Drill a hole in the center of the skullcap, making sure it's larger than the threads of the screws you will be using, and then anchor the antlers to the form with a single screw. Beginning at the center line, check for alignment and then check to assure the distance from the eye socket is the same as the original skull

Proper antler attachment is key. First, mark the centerline of the skullcap, easily located by the demarcation in the skull. The form will have a corresponding ridge, and it's important to align the two.

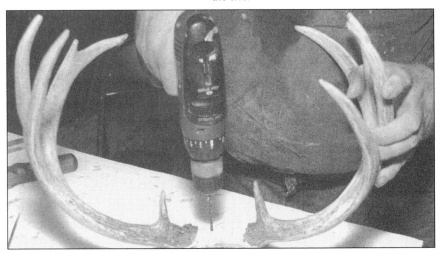

In the center of the skullcap, bore a hole larger than the screws being used.

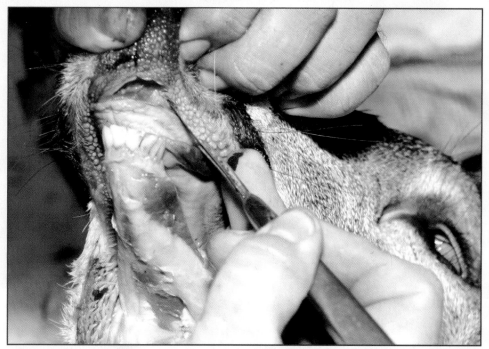

Some taxidermists, like Mark Nash, prefer to start caping with the lips. This way, you can see your cuts better as you follow the gum line.

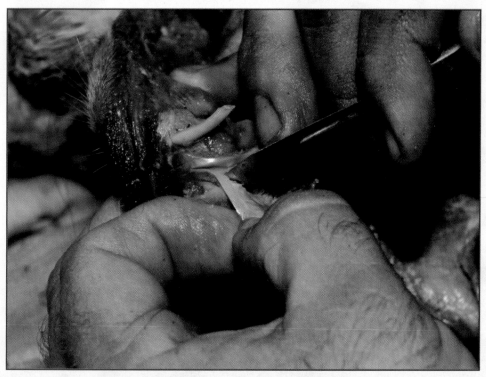

When fleshing the hide, be sure to remove the cartilage from the nostrils.

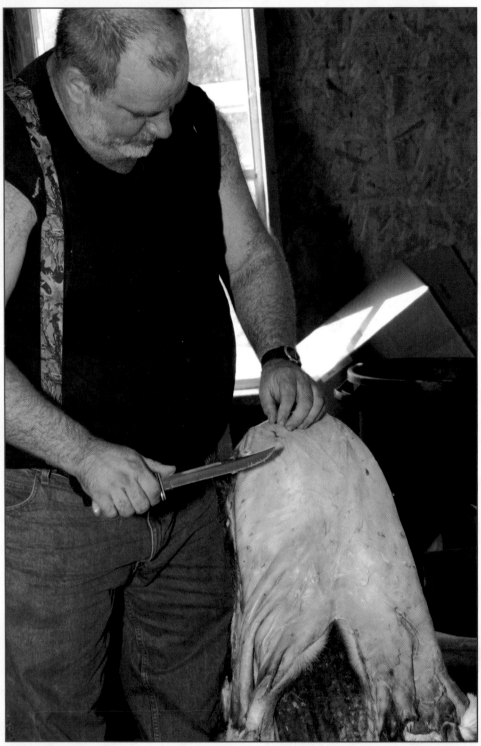

Prior to tanning the hide, you need to thin the cape to a uniform thickness so that it will tan evenly. You can use a fleshing knife with the hide on a fleshing beam, or use a wire wheel in an electric drill.

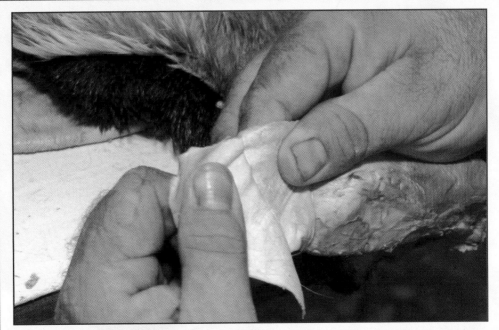

During the fleshing stage, all cartilage should be removed from the ears. Using a sharp scalpel, cut across the center of the cartilage of the ear but not through the skin. The two halves of the cartilage can then be peeled and carefully cut away from the skin.

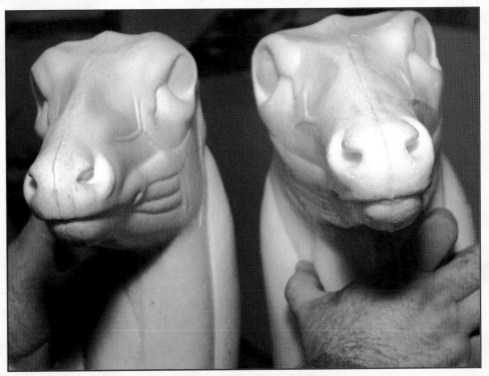

It is not only important to select the correct size head form, but also the proper regional form as well.

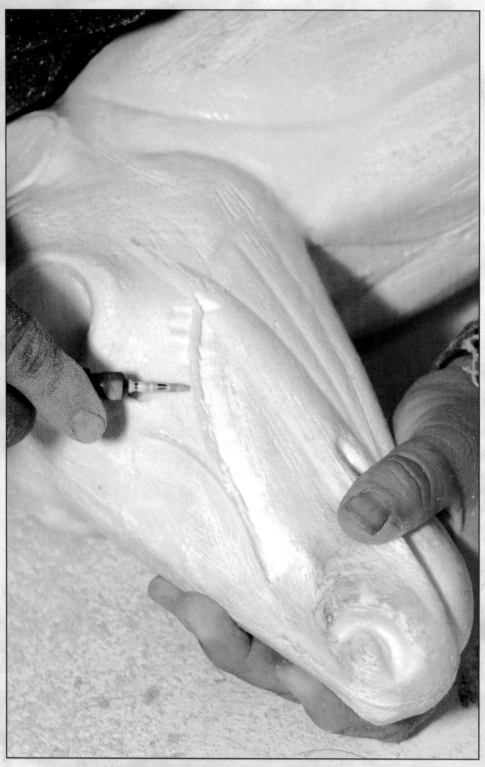

A tool like a Dremel will help accentuate facial details like veining.

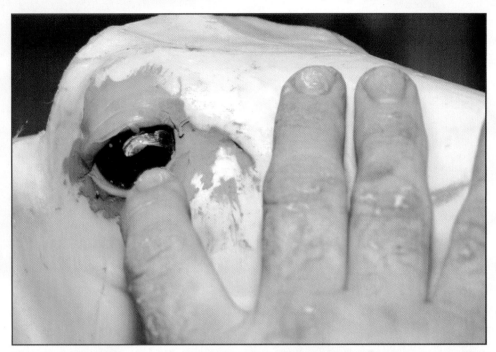

The eye capsule should be adhered to the manikin with hot glue and then clay should be applied around the upper and lower lids. All clay should be feathered out to make a smooth joint with the manikin.

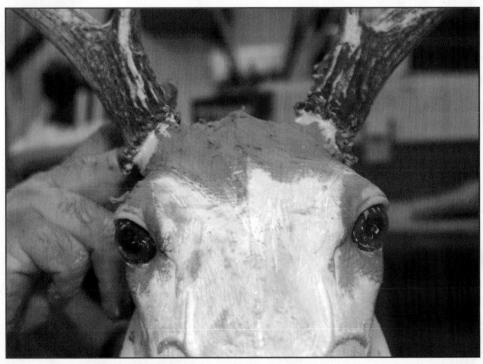

Clay is also used around the antler bases and skull cap. Make sure to use enough clay to smooth and fill out the form and build a realistic base on which the hide will sit.

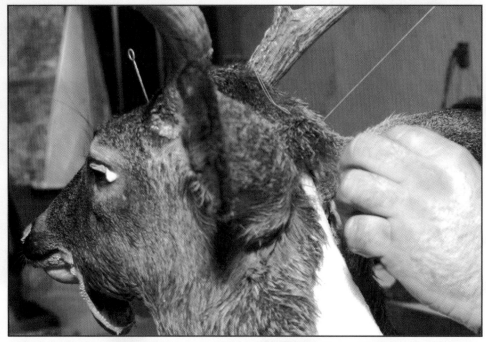

A baseball stitch is used to sew the hide together. After the hide is sewn around the antler bases, continue stiching down the back of the neck.

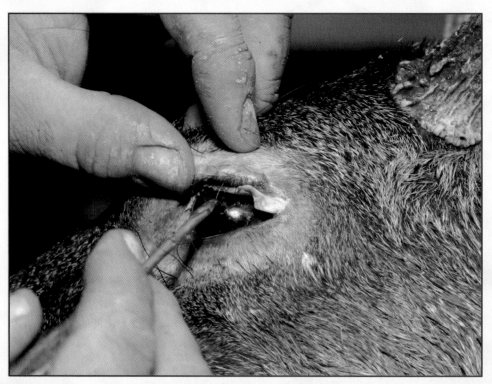

After the cape is sewn on, the skin around the eyes is tucked back under the clay and against the eye.

The nose and nostrils should also be painted. The front outside of the nose is usually painted with flesh or burnt umber colored paint. Black paint is then stippled on the front of the nose after the first coat has been painted. A semi-gloss finish will give the nose a "wet" look.

Once the hide is properly fitted and sewn down the back, it is secured with heavy-duty staples or upholstery tacks. Trim off any excess hide to ensure a smooth back area.

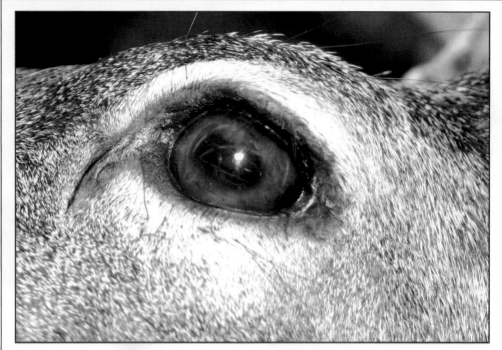

This is a finished eye. Note that the hide around the eye has been painted, beginning with burnt umber and then blended with black.

Cardboard and clamps are used to hold the ear straight while the glue and clay hardens, so the edges don't curl.

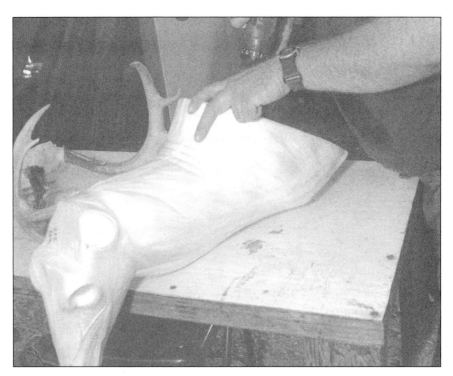

At this point, use lag screws to attach the form to a mounting stand or some other type of holder.

Regardless of the method used to hold the form, it must now be leveled. Use a small carpenter's level held against the form backboard to make sure it is plumb.

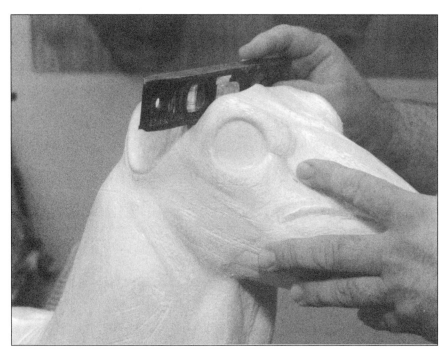

Then use the carpenter's level to make sure the form is level sideways, so you can visually check the antler position.

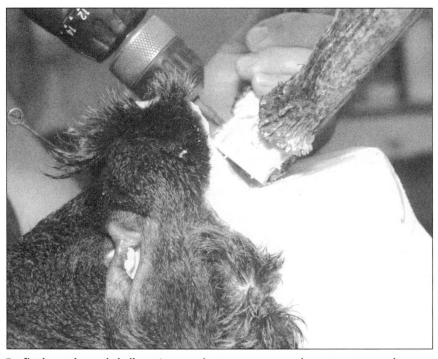

Try-fit the antler and skullcap. In some instances, you may have to cut some bone or shape the form for the antlers to fit properly.

measurement. At this time, you may wish to use a small carpenter's level on the back of the form to make sure the board is plumb and the angle of the antlers will be correct when the mount is hung on the wall. This will also be extremely important in setting the eyes. If a correction is needed, use a saw to cut the skullcap or a rasp to reshape the form to achieve the correct angle. In most instances, this won't be a problem. Once you're satisfied with the positioning, drill two more holes, one on either side of the center hole, and anchor the antler and skullcap in place.

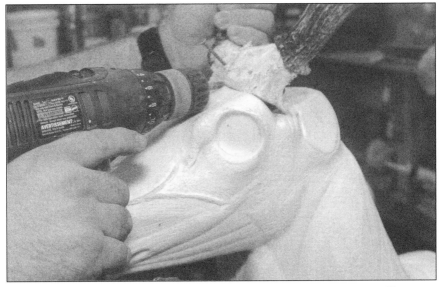

Once satisfied with the antler location, fasten them in place with three self-starting screws driven through pre-drilled holes in the skullcap and into the form.

Some kits provide papier-mâché to fill in around the antler and skullcap. If this is the case, the papier-mâché is mixed with water to a stiff consistency and placed in position, then roughly modeled with a tongue depressor, thin wooden stick or spatula. Mark Nash prefers to leave the antlers anchored but not filled in at this point, as he uses clay to build up just before installing the cape.

FYI, Rinehart Brain Ridge forms automatically align antlers correctly; no shims, wedges or rebuilding necessary.

11
Eye Modeling

One of the most important facets of a good deer-head mount, or any mount for that matter, is proper placement and modeling of the eyes. Poor eye placement and modeling can make a mount look unrealistic or, in some cases, downright terrible.

This is the most problematic area for beginners. Not only must the eyes be placed properly, but the modeling around them is what creates expression, whether you want to show calmness, fear or anger. For this reason, a wide range of plastic and glass eyes and eye treatments are available, glass being the better choice.

To help create more realistic eyes, taxidermist supply companies have also devised different "eye systems," such as Rinehart's pre-set eyes, which can be a great help to first-timers. Van Dyke's Synchron-Eye

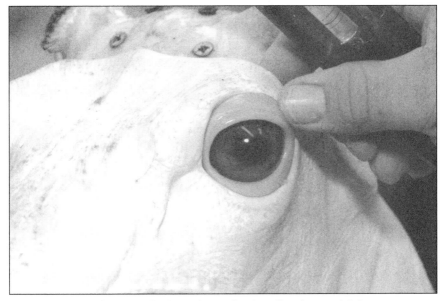

Several different methods can be used to install and/or model the eyes.

Capsules™ include the eye and a flexible eye capsule that holds it properly when positioned in a form's eye socket. When used with Van Dyke's Pre-Rotated II Eyes, the eyes can be manipulated to indicate the direction of the deer's gaze. For a deer

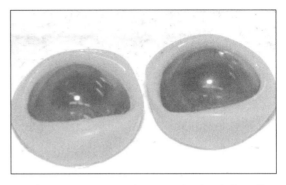

Synchron-Eyes come with a capsule that helps align the eye properly.

looking right, the eye is inserted in the capsule so that the white portion shows in the front corner of the right eye and the back corner of the left eye. To give the appearance of an intent forward look, both eyes are inserted with the white showing in the back corner of each. Synchron-Eye™ Capsules can be used in any manikin by simply drilling the eye socket with a one and one-half-inch spade bit and inserting the capsule in the socket. (It's okay to increase the diameter, as long as you don't increase the depth of the eye socket.) The Breakthrough Sportsman Series Dahmes Manikins (sculpted by Sallie

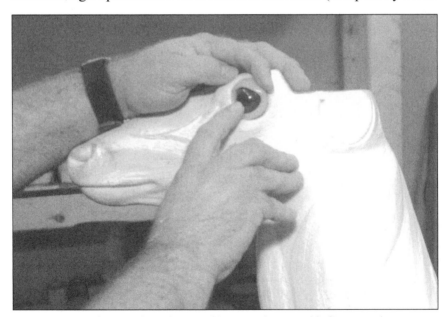

Insert the capsule and eye, making sure the assembly fits properly.

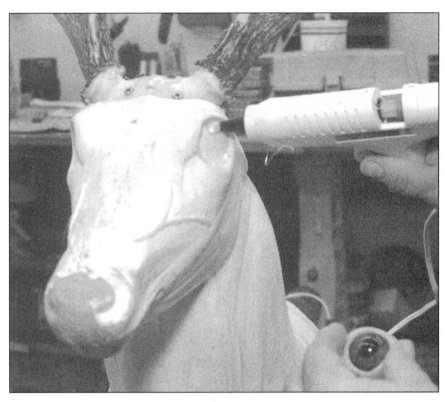

Use a hot-glue gun to anchor the eye capsule in place.

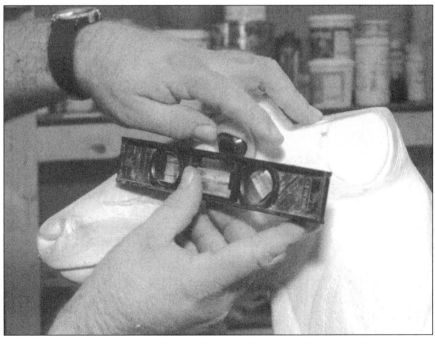

Immediately use a small carpenter's level to assure the pupil is level.

A flashlight may be necessary to check for level with some dark eyes.

Dahmes, from WASCO) come with eye orbits pre-set at the correct forty-five-degree forward angle and eleven-inch downward angle.

After mounting a deer head or two, you may wish to try more variations in head positions and eye positions. Just remember that a good eye reference is a must. Mark Nash has a head form reference that shows a full-open alert eye and a more normal eye, and he uses it religiously.

No matter what eye-setting method you use, always make certain that the back of the form is

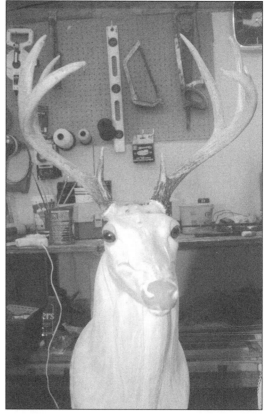

Install the opposite eye capsule and check to make sure both eyes align and are positioned evenly.

112

plumb. Then position the eye in the socket and use a carpenter's level to check that the pupil is level (Mark suggests using a flashlight on some dark eyes so you can see the pupil well) and to assure that both eyes are level with each other as seen from the front.

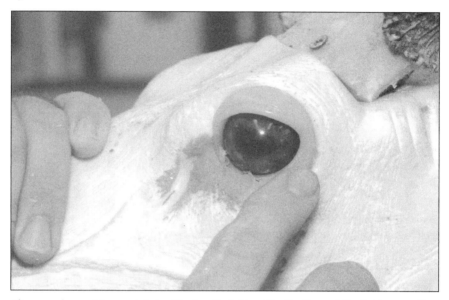

The capsule must be modeled with clay. First, blend in the lines of the bottom portion with the form.

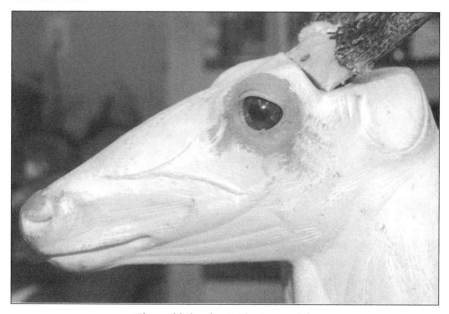

Then add the clay to the top eyelid.

In most instances, additional clay should be brought down to create a more natural top eyelid. All clay should be feathered out to a smooth joint with the manikin.

CLAY-SET EYES

Clay modeling is the traditional method for setting the eyes. They're placed in position, leveled and clay is molded around each eye to keep it in place. On some deeper-socket manikins, a small piece of clay is put in the socket first to hold the eye in place. Mark Nash likes to determine the eye position, use a glue gun to place a bit of hot glue in the eye socket before adding the clay, and then use more clay to fill in and around the eye and socket and level out the area. If using this method, you'll have to wet your fingers occasionally to help smooth and feather out the clay.

The upper and lower eyelids are then modeled with clay—and here's where you can really get creative. Make a small roll of clay about 3/16-inch in diameter and long enough to "arc" over the upper portion of the eye. Position the roll over the upper portion of the eye and, with some judicious placement and modeling of the lid, you can create different expressions using photos or three-dimensional references to get the right look. One important thing to remember is that a white-tail eye is oval, not round, so for the sake of realism, model the eyes to that shape.

Once you have this initial roll of clay in place, smooth it down with a modeling tool or your fingers and make a smaller roll to fill in above it. Smooth these two rolls together and use a modeling tool to create the crease in the upper lid. Again, use a reference to make sure this is correctly positioned.

Finally, create another small, 3/16-inch roll and place it in position for the lower eyelid. Shape it with a modeling tool, again using a reference. Smooth out all corners, feather the edges of the clay into the form and use the modeling tool to remove any clay from the eye. Repeat the process for the other eye. Finally, use a pair of calipers to measure the eyes and make sure they both have the same opening and position.

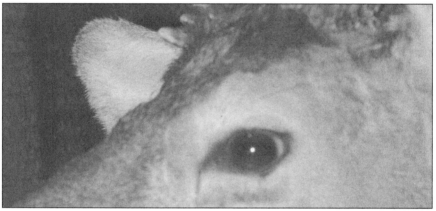

Eyes without eye forms require modeling, but they are also the most commonly used. It's important to make sure the eye fits the socket properly.

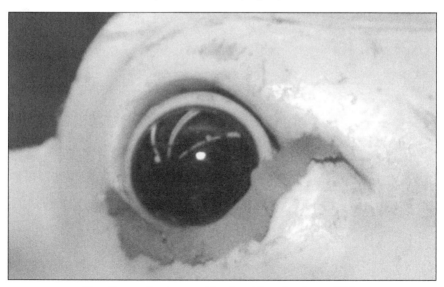

Glue the eye in place and begin adding the clay to fill in.

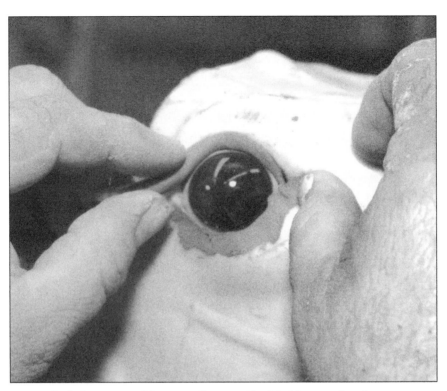

Both the upper and lower portions must be filled in around each eye.

This area must then be smoothed out onto the surrounding manikin surface.

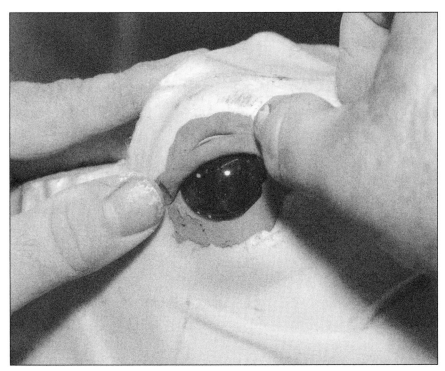

The upper and lower lids are now created. Carefully position a small roll of clay for the upper lid.

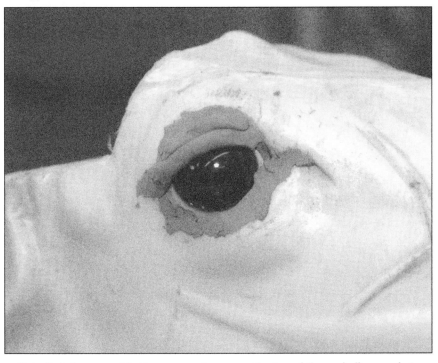

Note that the upper lid often comes down over the top of the eyeball somewhat.

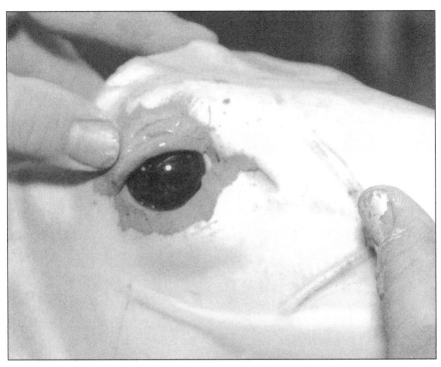

Smooth out the upper edge to the manikin, leaving the lid edge pronounced.

A correctly modeled upper lid.

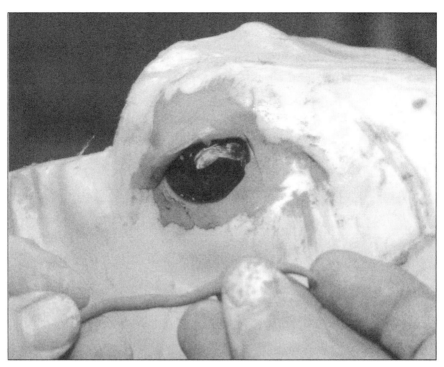

Create another small roll of clay and position it for the lower lid.

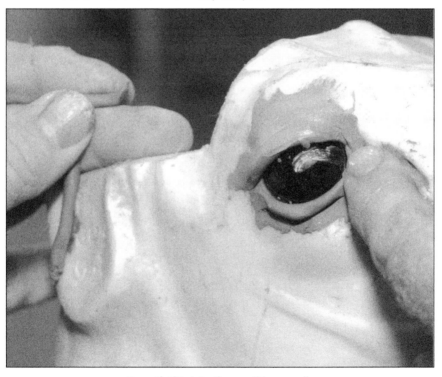

Smooth this into the manikin as well.

EYE SYSTEMS

To set Van Dyke's Synchron-Eyes™, slide the eyes into the capsules, level them by aligning the pupils with index marks on the back of the capsules. Place the right and left eye capsules into the proper eyes of the manikin, blending each of them in with a very small roll of clay on both top and bottom, and then modeling each eye crease.

With Rinehart "pre-molded" eye manikins, the eyes are already installed and you create the expression you desire by removing form material in the front or back corner of the eyes. If you would like the eye rotated to the side (away from the nose), you trim some of the

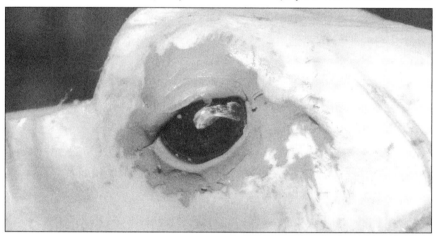

The resulting eyelids.

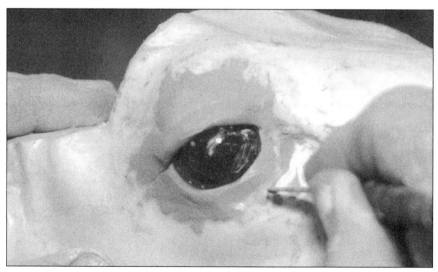

Use a modeling tool to finish, smooth, and sculpt the lids.

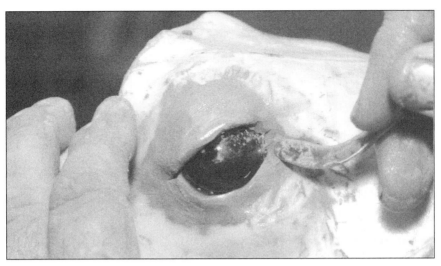

Make sure the clay doesn't extend down into the tear duct.

material away from the inside corner of the eye (near the tear duct). If you would like the eye rotated toward the nose, you trim some material away from the back corner of the eye. Although the pre-set eye has a molded eyelid, you may wish to enhance it using a rotary tool such as a Dremel. Press the hide into the deepened slot, deepening the tear duct slot as well for a more natural look. You will need to press clay into the slot to help hold the hide in place and to model the tear duct.

If at this point you're not ready to mount the cape onto the form immediately, cover the head with plastic food wrap to prevent the clay from drying out.

Mounting the Cape

Now comes the part you've been waiting for. In most instances, the hardest, most time-consuming chores are over. The actual mounting of the cape is relatively easy and doesn't take a particularly long time. The task does require attention to detail, however. The cape should be soft and flexible, somewhat damp but not wringing wet, and the form should be prepared and ready.

12

Fitting the Cape and Ear Liners

B efore you proceed, you need to try-fit the cape on the form. Mark Nash likes to leave off the clay around the antlers until the cape is ready for this step. He places the clay, smoothes it out and try-fits the cape, positioning it in place to determine if the eye and nose locations are correct. If you have the proper form, there should be no problem with this. Once you have the face skin correctly positioned, stick a T-pin through the skin in the middle of the forehead to temporarily hold the hide in place as you take other measurements.

The next fitting test should be around the antler bases. Pull the hide tight up into and under the antler burrs and make sure it will fit.

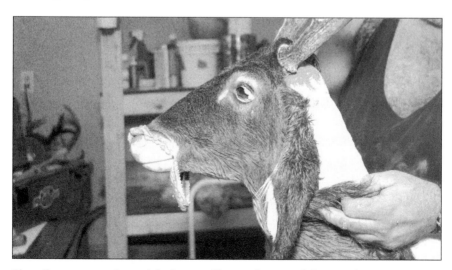

Place the cape over the upright form and locate the eyes. If the cape fits, use a T-pin to secure the cape in place.

You may have to remove the T-pin and readjust the face skin to fit the nose, eyes and antler burrs, and you may also have to reposition the antlers, taking material away from the form or adding clay to fill in.

Make sure the cape will fit over the neck. In the illustration shown, the form was designed for a swelled neck and the cape was too narrow. Foam material had to be cut away from the back and sides of the neck to correct the problem. In most instances, however, it's best not to do anything beyond some minor shaving or trimming of the form. Temporarily press the cape into the muscular modeling to determine the final

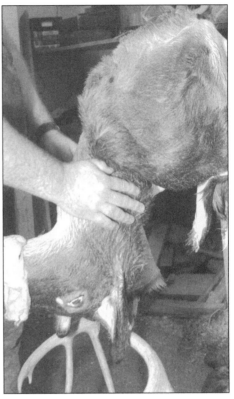

Turn the form upside-down and make sure the neck and brisket areas fit.

detail shape, and always check to see that there is enough cape to cover the brisket and shoulders.

PREPARING THE CAPE

Any bullet holes, knife cuts or other problems with the cape should be sewn or corrected at this point. A better looking repair on a bullet hole can be done by first lengthening the hole into an elongated slit it's much better to gather the material in a line rather than have it "bunch up" Near a round hole. If Mark Nash has a cape that has been cut completely up the back of the neck, he sews the lower portion together from the inside so that less of the seam is revealed, and he sews the hide up to about six inches below the "Y." "Like a zipper, it's important to start the two ends together properly," Mark says. He recommends a basic lock stitch used for sewing these repairs from the flesh side. It produces a very sturdy but easily concealed seam.

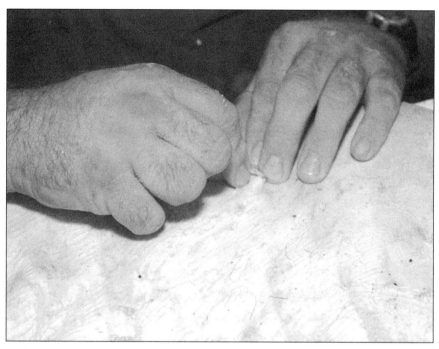

The cape must be prepared by repairing any bullet holes, bad cuts or other flaws.

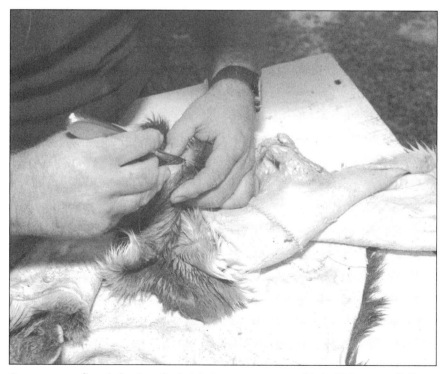

One common flaw is having the brisket area cut up too high. Make sure all flaws are repaired.

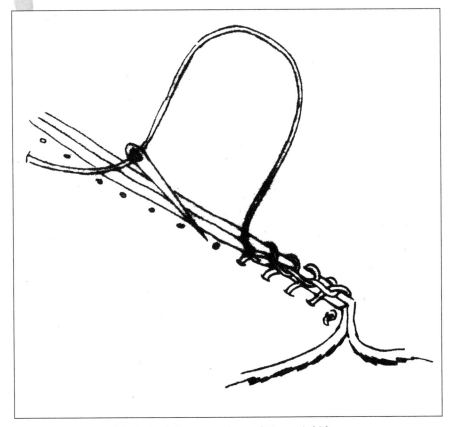

A lock stitch is commonly used to repair hides.

INSTALLING EAR LINERS

You'll probably be using commercial ear liners, and these should also be try-fitted. As with the eye systems, manufacturers have devised ear systems that are fairly easily installed and natural-looking. You should have already decided whether you will use forward facing or back positioned ears, and liners are available for both in small, medium and large, since purchasing the correct size simplifies things. These days, ear liners such as those from WASCO, Rinehart and Van Dyke are extremely realistic, with veining on the back that stands out on short-haired capes or those trophies taken in early bow season.

With the ears still turned inside out, sprinkle borax over the surface to soak up any tanning creams that may still remain. Then lightly rough the skin on the backside of the ear. Note: Many taxidermists keep the lower cartilage attached, which helps give the ears a more natural appearance.

Next, insert the ear liner into the ear to try-fit it. You may have to thin the edges of some liners to fit properly. A Dremel tool can be used to do this quickly and make any other modifications needed. Go carefully at this stage and try-fit several times until you get a natural-looking ear, with the liner fitting perfectly.

Now it's time to glue the liners in place. Most ear liner manufacturers suggest washing the ear liner in lacquer thinner to remove the mold release agent and slightly

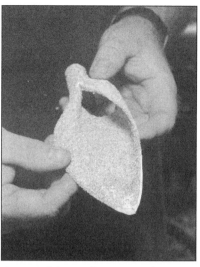

Commercial ear liners are the most common method of creating the ears.

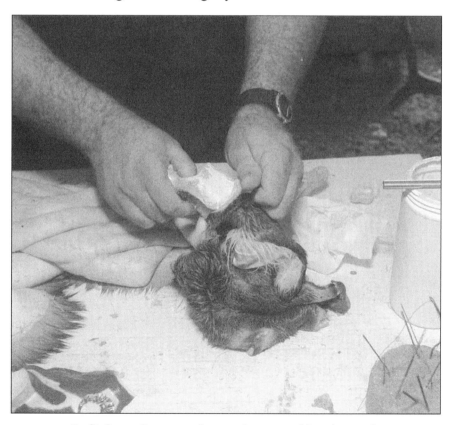

Try-fit the ear liners to make sure they are positioned correctly.

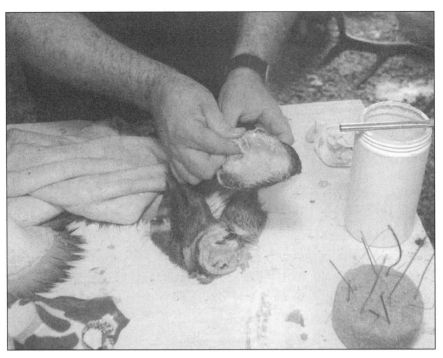

Make sure the liners come out to the full edge of the ears.

If the liners fit in place, lightly roughen them with sandpaper, then coat them with ear-glue or hide-glue.

roughen the surface. The ear liner should also be slightly roughened with sandpaper. Nash dips the ear liner in lacquer thinner, and then places it in the ground corn cobs or sawdust used for degreasing birds and other skins. Once the lacquer thinner has dried, tiny pieces are bonded to the plastic, creating a fairly rough surface that holds the glue extremely well.

Apply Ear Epoxy Earliner or any other ear liner adhesive you've chosen, or mix hide paste to a stiff consistency and paint it on the ear liners. Slide the liners back in place and position them properly. Some taxidermists add a tiny bit of clay in the tip of the ear, which allows for better shaping of the edge.

Carefully shape the ear, pressing the hide in place, and use a small brush to comb the hair. This not only presents a better-looking mount, but the pressure helps the hide stick to the liner. Many taxidermists also like to place a couple of staples in the base of the ear to help hold the hide in place and prevent "drumming," or the contraction of the skin, which pulls it away from concave surfaces. Once the ears have set, the staples can be removed if they're visible. If they're not visible, leave them in place.

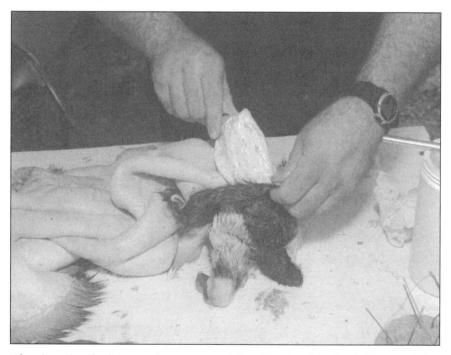

When inserting the liners, make sure you get the right liner into the right ear and the left into the left ear.

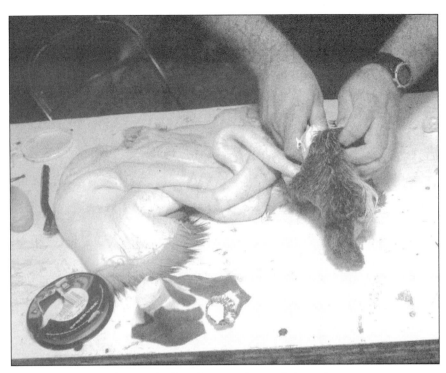

Make sure the liner is pressed properly into place.

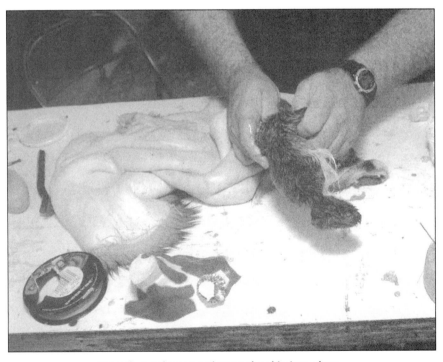

Smooth out the ear and press the skin into place.

The next step is to build up the ear butt. Again, a good reference is invaluable, and a commercially made ear butt model can be an excellent reference. Some taxidermists like to build up and model the ear butts while the cape is lying flat on a table, which provides a means of matching the ear shapes. Some use bonding materials to build up the ear butt; others, like Mark Nash, use clay. Nash rough-shapes the ear butts, and then mounts the cape, continuing to shape and reshape the ear butt after the cape is in place. Regardless of

Use a stiff-bristle brush to firmly groom and press both the inside and outside skin in place around the liner. Put clay in the ear butts to hold the liners in position and fill out the ears.

which way you work, keep combing and brushing the hair as you shape the ear butt so you can see the results and create a more natural-looking ear.

Finally, examine the cape one last time to make sure it is ready for mounting.

At this point the fun really begins as you finally see your mount take shape. This is also the time to proceed very slowly and carefully and enjoy the task.

13
Mounting the Skin

Mark Nash likes to place a bit of clay around the nose and lips to allow for more detailed modeling, and he also inserts a thin layer of clay into the nostrils. He then applies hide paste to the face, around the back of the head and down the neck slightly, but not to the entire form. This allows you to work on facial details before you have to work the neck, brisket and shoulder areas. With the paste applied, reposition the cape in place, again aligning the face and making sure the nose, eyes and areas around the antler bases are exactly where they should be. When you're satisfied with the positioning again, anchor the cape in place with a T-pin through the center of the forehead.

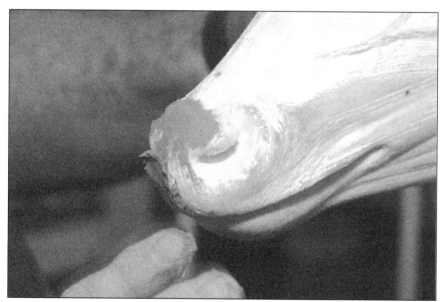

A thin layer of clay is applied around the front of the nose and in the nostrils and in the tear ducts as well.

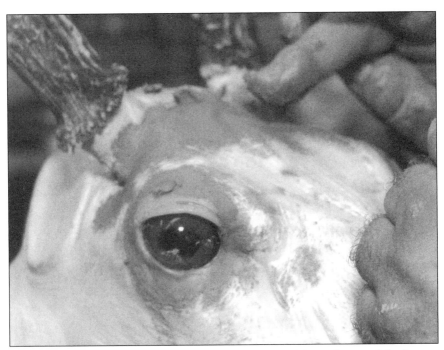

Clay is applied around the skullcap and antler bases to fill out the top of the form.

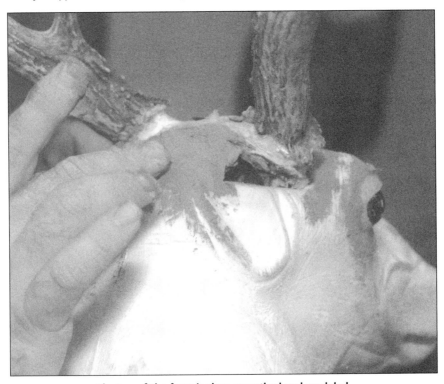

The top of the form is then smoothed and modeled.

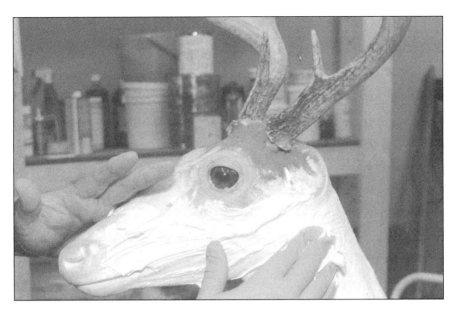

Hide glue is applied to the face, top of the head, and around the upper neck areas

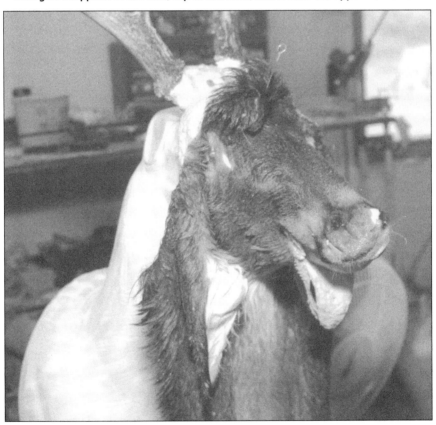

The cape is then placed over the face and aligned with the eyes.

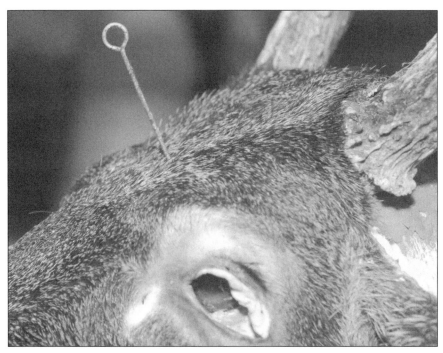

A T-pin is used to hold the cape in place.

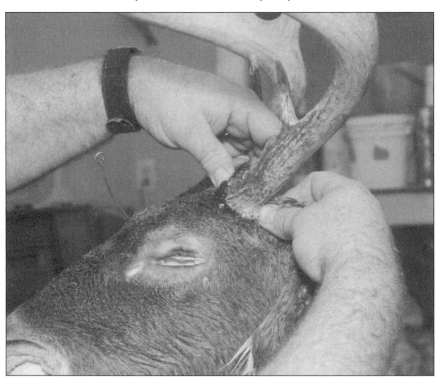

Make sure the cape fits properly around the antler bases.

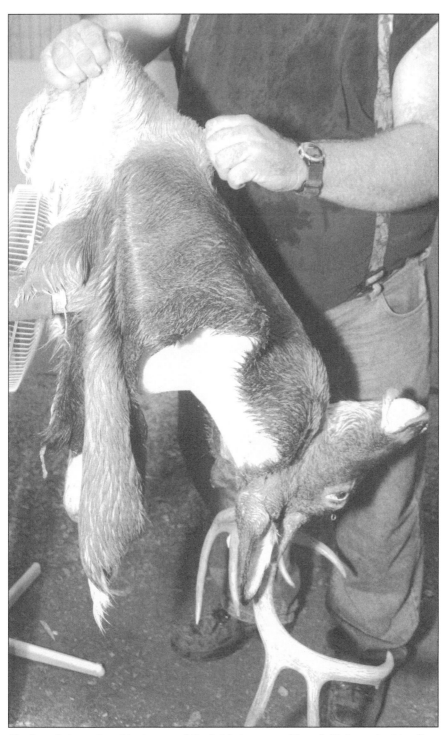

The form is turned upside-down and the brisket area positioned. It's important to align and match the crest of the brisket to the crest on the form. Again, T-pins are used to temporarily hold the cape in place.

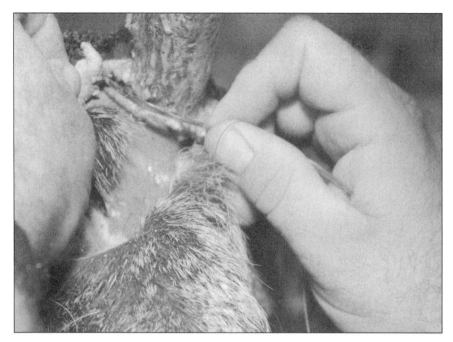

The fastening of the cape begins at the antler bases. Pull the cape up around the antler bases and begin stitching.

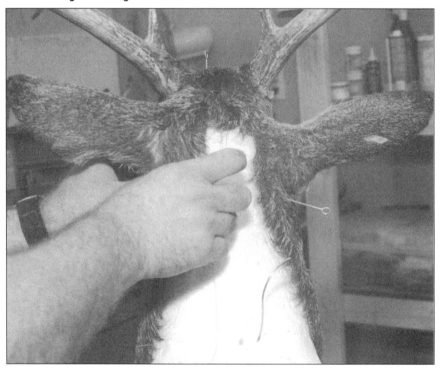

If more or less clay is needed, model so the cape fits well around the antlers. Then continue stitching the "Y" cut down the neck.

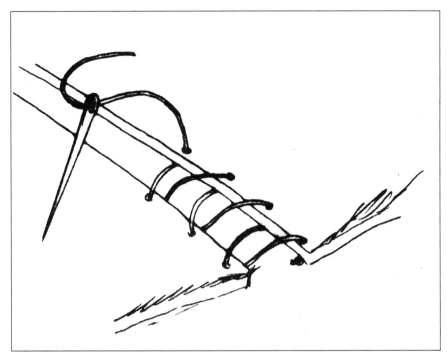

Use a baseball stitch to fasten the hide together.

Turn the form upside-down and fold the hide over the brisket and down the back of the form board. Check the positioning again and, as needed, adjust carefully at this time. Make sure that the large "V" of long hair, located in the center of the brisket, fits the corresponding V-shape in the form. Press the hide in place to make sure it will fit properly, and use a couple of T-pins to temporarily hold the cape where you want it.

Turn the form right-side up and make sure the cape is still correctly positioned. Like many taxidermists, Nash prefers to start checking for position at the lips and, if they and the nose fit properly, he begins sewing the "Y" together at each antler base using a simple baseball stitch, but only sewing enough to gather the cape around the antlers. This further "anchors" the cape in place for the other detail work.

TUCKING EYES

The eyes are tucked next and once again, a good photographic reference is extremely important. The first step is to locate the tear duct slot in

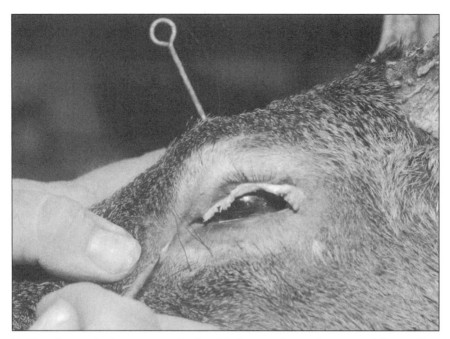

Tucking the eyes is the next step. Begin with the tear duct and use a modeling tool or small screwdriver to tuck the hide into the slot. You may wish to pin this in place, concealing the pin by pushing it into the hide.

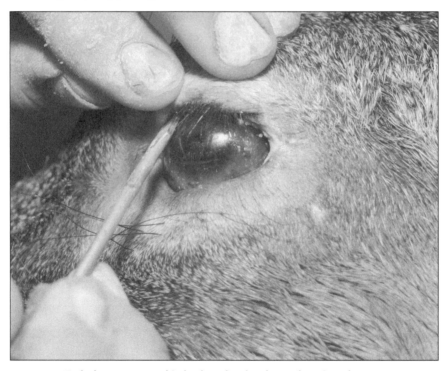

Tuck the upper eye skin back under the clay and against the eye.

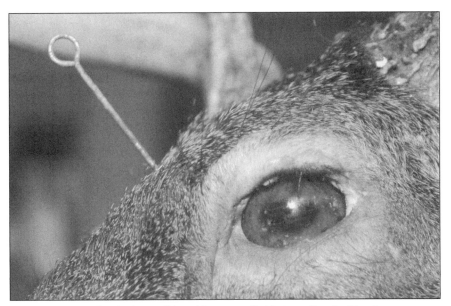

Repeat for the lower lid, making sure all skin is well tucked in place.

front of one eye and, using a modeling tool or the end of a small screwdriver, tuck the hide into the slot. You can pin this in place temporarily, although some taxidermists like to pin this area permanently, pushing the pin all the way in and concealing it in the finishing. Tuck the upper eye skin back in and under the clay (between the clay and the eye) and repeat for the lower eye skin, tucking it in securely between the clay roll and the eyeball. This will cause the clay to become somewhat misshaped, but you can use the modeling tool to remodel the lids around the eye.

Once you have the hide tucked and the eyes reshaped, use a modeling tool to put the crease back in the upper lid. This crease is easily seen on the hide. Just follow the slight crease in the skin, pushing it down in a groove made in the clay. Nash likes to push a fine pin in place in the front of the eye, and some taxidermists will use two permanent pins pushed into the hide to be concealed. Use the blunt end of a small screwdriver to force them in place. Taxidermists also sometimes pin the back of the eye, but it usually isn't necessary.

Use a small, fine artists brush to brush away any clay from the eyeball and to clean the area. Repeat for the opposite eye and then stand back and look at the face from the front to make sure the eyes match. Adjust as needed.

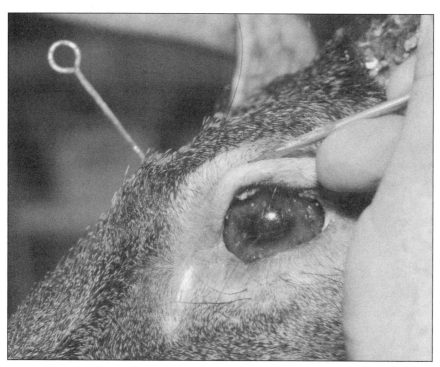

Use a modeling tool to place the crease in the upper eyelid.

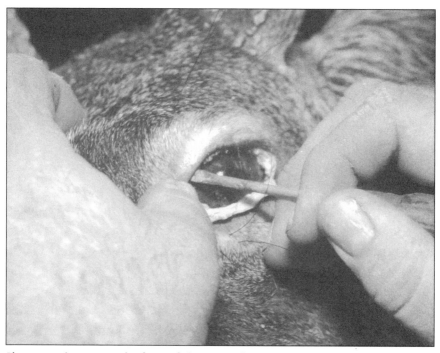

Place two pins, one at the front of the eye and one at the rear, to hold the eye skin permanently in place.

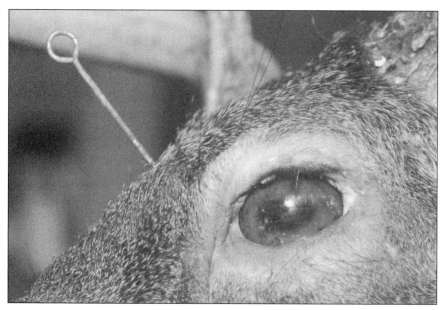

The resulting eye. Repeat the steps on the other eye, making sure you have them tucked and modeled to match.

TUCKING NOSTRILS

It's now time to tuck the nostrils. First, locate the groove in the center of the nose, and push it into the clay that lightly covers the nose. Then tuck the nose skin into the clay you've placed inside the nasal cavities. If the skin needs some trimming to tuck properly, use a sharp scalpel to make sure it fits correctly. Nash usually places a small pin in the front of the nostril to help hold the skin in place, and conceals the pin by pushing it in with a screwdriver blade. Paper towel pieces can also be wadded up and pushed into the nasal passage to help hold the skin in place until the glue dries and the clay sets up.

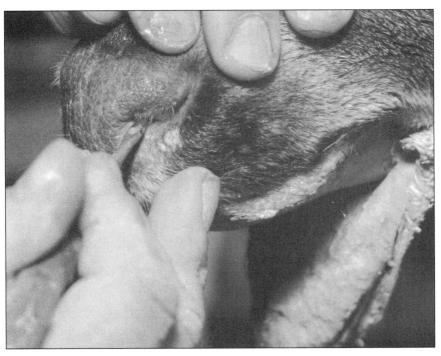

To tuck the nostrils, first locate the center groove in the nose and press it lightly into the clay covering the nose. Then tuck the nose skin into the clay you've placed inside the nostrils.

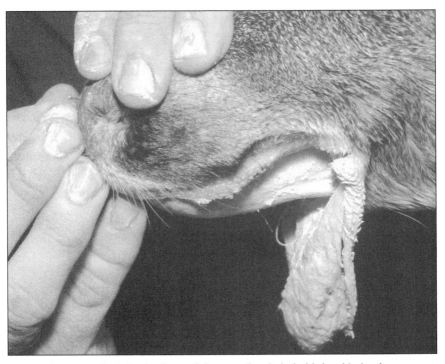

Place a small pin in the front of the nostril to help hold the skin in place.

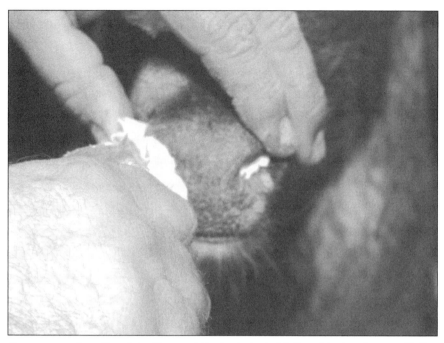

Press paper toweling into the nostrils to help hold the skin in place until the glue and clay sets.

TUCKING LIPS

Turn the form over or upside down so you can see the lips and tuck the top lip in place, again using a small screwdriver or modeling tool. Start in one corner and push lightly, moving around toward the front. Go to the opposite corner and come around to meet again at the front. Note that the corners will need more material tucked in, but this lets you tuck the lip skin in place evenly and then go back and fix the excess corner skin.

Mark Nash likes to place a small ball of clay inside the front edge of the bottom lip skin before tucking it in place, smoothing and rounding the clay to create a more "filled" bottom lip, which may otherwise look shrunken. Nash also puts a pin or two in the lower lip. These can be left in place and painted over in the finishing steps.

SHAPING AND POSITIONING EARS

Turn the manikin right-side up and begin positioning the ears to suit. You may have to add more clay to the ear butts to create the fullness needed, or you may have to remove some clay. Again, work very

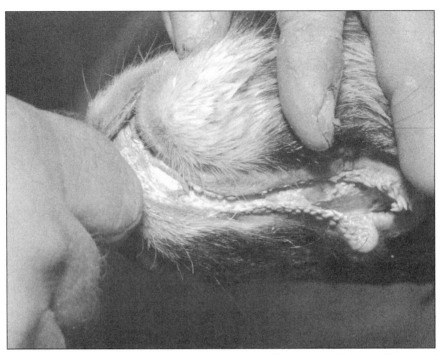

Turn the form upside-down and tuck the lower lip in place, again using a modeling tool or the end of a small screwdriver.

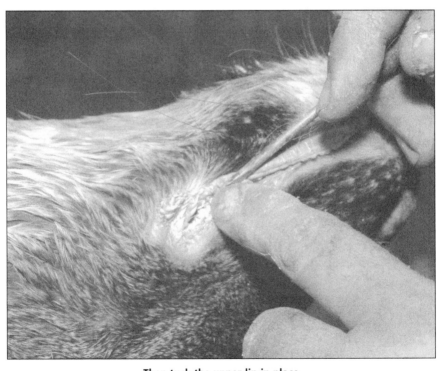

Then tuck the upper lip in place.

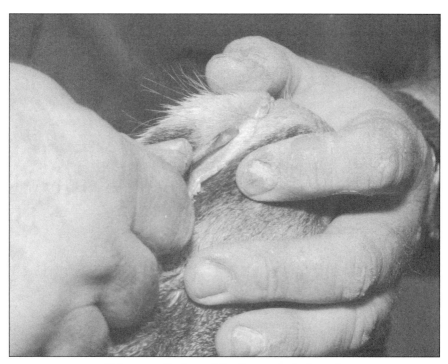

Make sure all edges of the lips are tucked evenly.

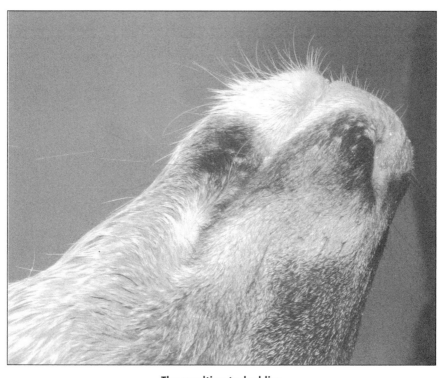

The resulting tucked lips.

With the manikin still upside-down, remove the temporary T-pin on the brisket and apply hide glue to the remainder of the form.

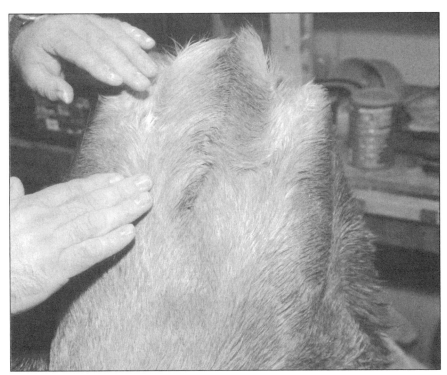

Again, relocate and position the brisket. Make sure the crests fit, pressing the indentations down in the crevices.

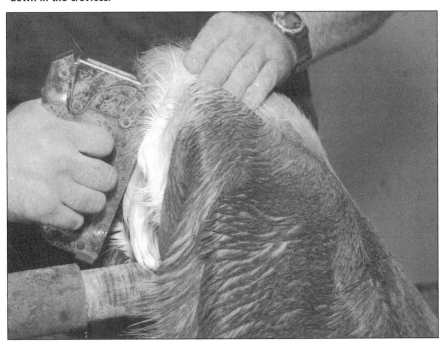

Fasten the hide to the backboard in the brisket area.

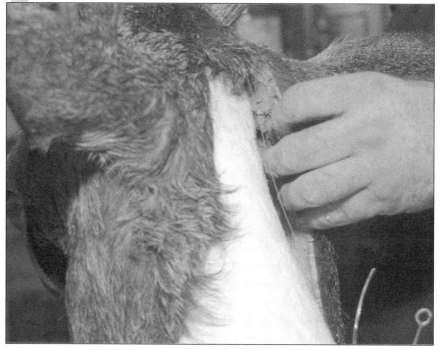

Turn the form upright and position the ears. You may need to add or remove clay from the ear butts.

carefully and make continual references to ear shape and position to create a natural-looking ear: turned forward denoting alertness, turned back to denote relaxation, turned down and back to simulate a "mad" demeanor (to simulate aggression). Or, they may be positioned in a non-similar fashion, say with one ear slightly back and the other further back. Once the clay is positioned, you can remove or add as you see fit.

Note there is often one crease, sometimes more than one, in front of the ear, between it and the antler base. Use your finger and a screwdriver or modeling tool to push the cape in and form the crease or creases. Once you get the ears in the proper position, you can hold them with fishing line, make holes in the ears and tie the line to T-pins on different parts of the form. Comb out the ears, and use cardboard and small clamps to keep the edges straight, if there seems to be any curling of the edges.

Since the cape isn't sewn together yet, this mounting procedure gives you the advantage of being able to remove and readjust the form or cape to suit.

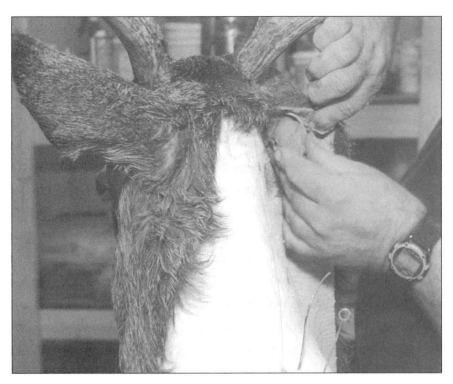

As you position the ears, continue sewing the "Y" or down the back of the neck.

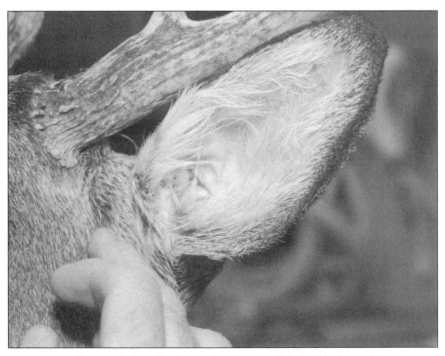

Use your finger to indent the "crease" or "creases" desired in front of the ears.

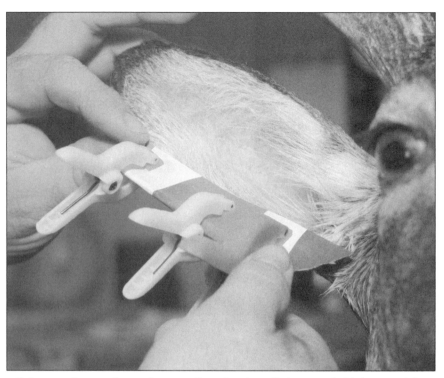

If the ear edges tend to curl, use cardboard and small clamps to hold them straight.

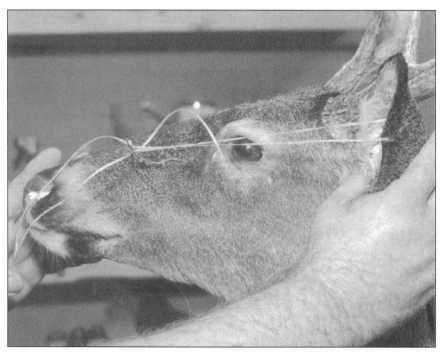

You may also need to wire or tape the ears in position until the glue and clay sets up.
Finish the remainder of the sewing.

ATTACHING THE CAPE

If you're satisfied with the facial expression, positioning and ears, you're ready to finish the remainder of the cape. Remove the T-pin in the brisket area and peel back the cape. Spread hide glue over the rest of the form and over any interior stitches, such as bullet holes or long neck closures in the cape.

Reposition the cape and find the proper location of the brisket V. Press the cape in place and make sure it fits well down into the small troughs on each side of the larger V. With staples or upholstery tacks, fasten the excess portion of the cape in that area to the backboard, being careful not to pull the cape up out of the hollows in the brisket, then sew up the back of the neck. If you're using the tube method with only a short Y opening, begin with the connection you've just made at the antler burrs and continue sewing the short sides of the Y

Fasten the rest of the cape to the backboard of the manikin with staples and trim where needed for a smooth fit.

down toward its bottom leg. Make the stitches about 1/4-inch apart and pull the seam together tightly, but do not allow it to gather or "bunch up."

As you stitch, continue to examine the ear butts. They may pull slightly out of place with the stitching and need to be repositioned. Using this method, you can continue to add or remove clay to reposition the ear butts right up until you reach the point where the top legs of the Y come together. If everything is in order, finish sewing down the bottom leg of the Y and tie the thread off. Then lightly pound down the seam with a rubber or wooden mallet. Once all sewing is finished, fasten the remainder of the excess cape on the back of the backboard with staples or upholstery tacks, and trim off excess hide with a sharp knife to create a smooth back area.

Remove any hide adhesive from the hair with the appropriate cleaner as directed by the adhesive manufacturer. Brush down all the hair, smoothing out any cowlicks and using long, fairly hard strokes to

Gently pound down the seam with a rubber hammer or wooden mallet, then remove any hide adhesive that may have gotten on the cape.

help push the cape in place in the muscling details. If the hair doesn't set properly while the cape is still wet, it will be almost impossible to smooth down, but you can use hair-setting gel to do the job. Some taxidermists pin a heavy cardboard strip along the top neck seam to keep the hair down in place until the cape dries. Many also like to pin around the antler burrs to prevent the cape from shrinking away in those areas. You can use finishing nails as well, cutting off the heads and driving them down into the skin after the cape has dried properly. Lastly, examine the face again to make sure everything is suitably positioned and secure.

Continue to watch the mount as it dries, checking it frequently each day and readjusting as necessary. You may have to pin other portions or even wrap them with gauze or cheesecloth to help hold things in place until the adhesive sets and the cape is completely dry.

Finishing

The finishing details are what make the taxidermist an "artist." The mount must be thoroughly dry before you begin the finishing, however, and this could take anywhere from a week to two or more weeks, depending on the humidity and drying temperature. Most taxidermists wait at least two weeks to make sure the mount has dried completely before they continue with the finishing process.

14

Cleaning, Filling, and Painting

Remove any supports, pins or other items that may be holding the cape in place and brush down the entire cape with a wire brush. Use an air compressor blowgun first to blow off dust and dirt that may have accumulated. Mark Nash likes to "back-brush," then he brushes the hair solidly in the right direction and,

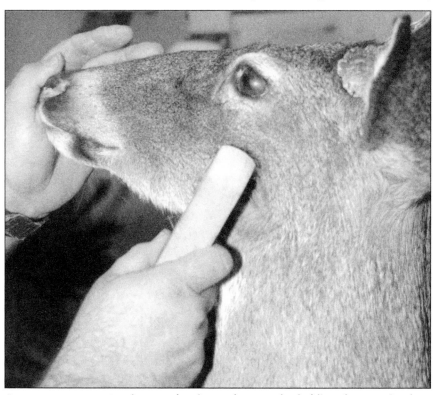

Remove any supports, pins or other items that may be holding the cape in place. Then back-brush the entire cape with a wire brush to fluff up the hair.

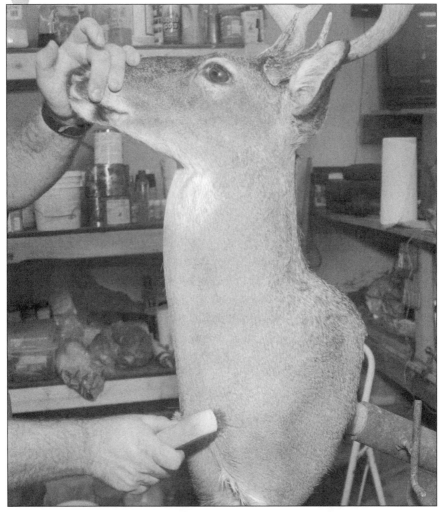

Using the wire brush, smooth the hair back down in the direction of the hair.

finally, smooths it down with the flat of his hand. Some taxidermists like to blow the hairs backward with the air gun, and then brush the hairs back smooth with the brush.

Brush and fluff out the ears. Whitetails have long hairs around the nose and face, and these hairs may have been "glued" in place with the setting gel. Pull them out and away from the hide and into their natural positions.

Examine the hide for any cracks, especially around the eyes, lips and nostrils. You may find that some shrinkage has occurred around the eyes. Lightly fill in any cracks or shrinkage using a filler such as Apoxie Sculpt. You may want to mix coloring into the material to aid

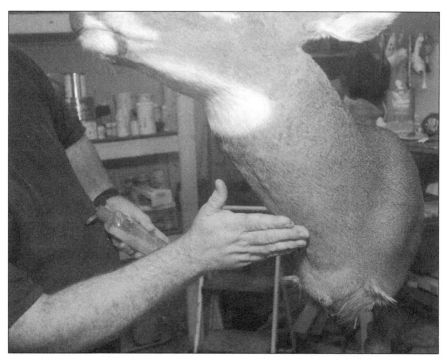

Finally, use your hands to rub the hair down as smooth as possible.

Brush and fluff out the ears. Note the rough-looking hair pattern of this unfinished ear.

Whitetails have long hairs under their chin and around the nose and face. Make sure these are straight and standing out properly.

in concealing the cracks. Use a modeling tool to fill in tiny cracks around the eyes, and between the lid and the eyeball. Then use a small-bristle brush to smooth the filler, making sure it's fairly thin in consistency. Fill in any pinholes in the eyes, nose and lips, and place just a bit of filler deep in the nostrils. Nash also likes to slightly fill in the upper and/or lower lip, making sure there is a definite lip line.

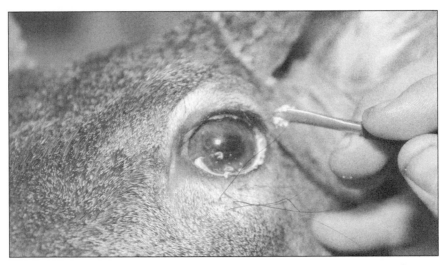

Fill any cracks around the eyes, lips, or nostrils with filler, such as Apoxie Sculpt.

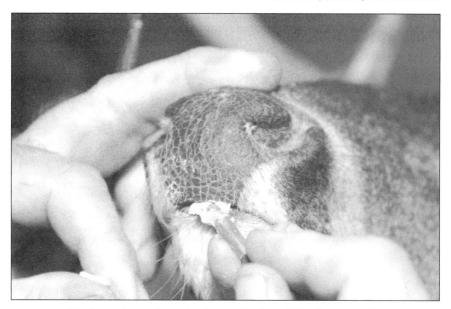

The lower lip tends to shrink, so add a bit of filler here as well.

Some taxidermists prefer to use beeswax to fill in cracks or shrunken areas. The Sallie Dahmes Finishing Wax is an excellent choice. Warm the wax with a light bulb and apply with a modeling tool. Smooth up the wax with lacquer thinner to create an even, smooth surface. Once all modeling and rebuilding has been done, apply a coat of fungicide such as Master Painter's fungicidal, or Polytranspar fungicidal sealer to any areas that will be painted.

Sallie Dahmes Finishing Wax from WASCO makes eye and nose finishing easy, even for first-timers. (PHOTO COURTESY WASCO)

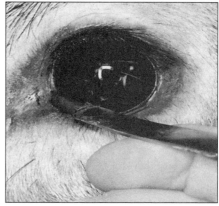

Shape a small amount of wax into a long, thin roll between your fingers. Place the wax on the lower eyelid and force it into the crease with a modeling tool. Repeat for the upper lid. (PHOTO COURTESY WASCO)

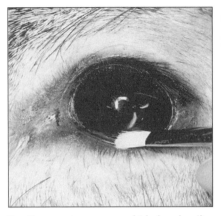

Use the wax to cover any hide head nails and to shape a nictitating membrane, smoothing the wax with lacquer thinner. Clean the glass eye with Windex. (PHOTO COURTESY WASCO)

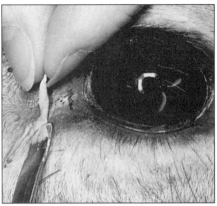

Place a small amount of Ivory White colored wax into the tear duct and shape it with a modeling tool. (PHOTO COURTESY WASCO)

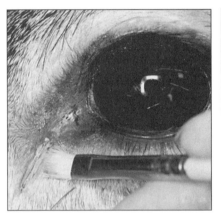

Blend the edges of the wax out of the tear duct and use a soft brush and lacquer thinner to smooth the wax. (PHOTO COURTESY WASCO)

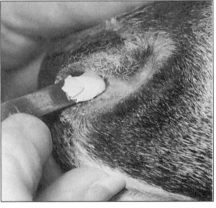

Place a small piece of flesh-colored wax deep into the nostril opening. Use a modeling tool to spread the wax inside the nostril. (PHOTO COURTESY WASCO)

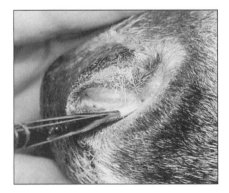

Feather the edges of the wax out to where the white hairs of the nostrils start. Smooth the wax with a paint brush and lacquer thinner (PHOTO COURTESY WASCO)

PAINTING AND HANGING

Many expert taxidermists use an airbrush for the painting details. This does require a compressor and airbrush along with the paints, and not a little practice to gain expertise. Many commercial taxidermists also

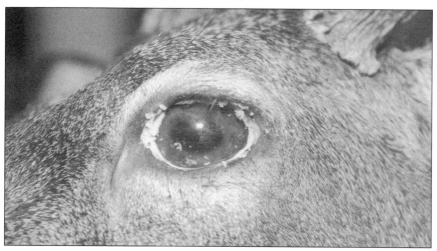

Painting is necessary to finish out the mount. Note the filled areas around the eyes.

prefer to use artist's oil paints such as those made by Windsor Newton—a range of colors that include: flesh pink, ivory, black, burnt umber, mars red and titanium white. You will also need an assortment of brushes, including stiff and soft bristle and at least one tiny "liner" brush, plus brush cleaner and thinner.

FINISHING THE EYE

Clean the eyes with Windex. Lightly brush burnt umber onto the skin surrounding each eye in a very thin band, thinning the oil paint as needed for easy application. Do not over paint. Apply a very tiny line of black to the skin touching the eye and brush a tiny bit of mars red into the crease of the tear duct. Then blend it in with the burnt umber—but don't overdo this color. Apply a little bit of flesh pink in the front corner of the eye, or mix burnt umber and mars red with titanium white to achieve the flesh coloring.

Mix a bit more of the white with just a little burnt umber, then use a stiff-bristle brush to blend and feather the white area of skin around the eyes. Continue gently blending and feathering the colors to create a natural look. Use lacquer thinner and a fine brush to clean any paint

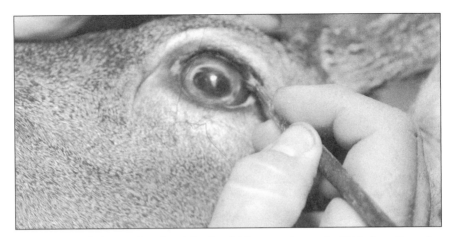

The area around the eyes is painted. Begin with burnt umber and add black on the outer edges, blending it all together.

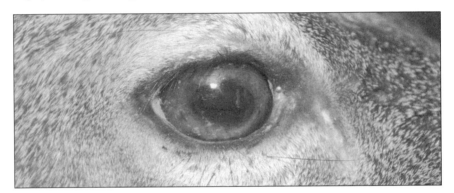

The finished eye.

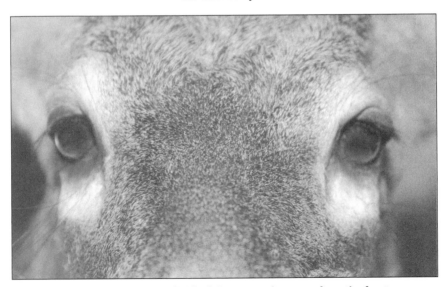

Make sure both eyes are finished the same when seen from the front.

from the eyeballs, allow the paint to dry thoroughly, and then clean the eyes again with Windex.

FINISHING THE NOSE AND LIPS

Paint a little flesh pink color in the interior of the nostril. Then apply a little white mixed with just a touch of burnt umber to the white hair inside the nostril to highlight the area. Mark Nash likes to "model" the nose by first applying a bit of burnt umber over the entire surface and then stippling the paint in place to get into all creases and crevices. He then applies a tiny bit of mars red to the underside of the upper lip, blending this in with the burnt umber. Finally, Nash brushes black over the top surface of the nose.

The lower lip is painted in much the same manner. Again, begin with the mars red on the crevice, add a line of burnt umber between the lips, followed by black, and then blend all the colors together.

Once the paint has dried, apply a semi-gloss or satin sheen varnish to the nose. Derma-Coat Nose/Hoof Clear is a special taxidermist material that can be used to create the "wet-look" nose.

The nose must also be painted. Note the coloration of the unfinished nose.

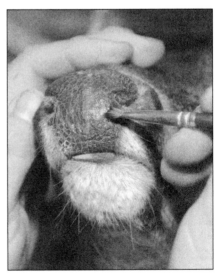

Paint a little flesh color into the nostrils.

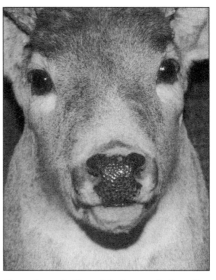

Then paint the front outside of the nose with flesh or burnt umber. Note that only one-half of this nose has been painted.

Black is then stippled over the first coat and gently rubbed in.

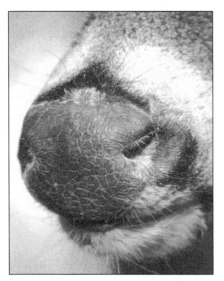

The finished painted nose.

Once the paint has dried, a semi-gloss finish can be applied to the nose to provide a "wet" look.

FINISHING THE EARS

Use a light coat of white oil paint on all the membrane areas inside the ears to bring out the color. Don't paint it on too heavily! Then go back in with flesh pink and add a few highlights, using more flesh pink in the deeper interior portion of the ear.

FITTING THE BACKBOARD AND HANGER

In many instances, a decorative backboard is installed over the back of the form, and if you have a band saw and router, you can easily make your own. The board should extend past the form board at least an inch all around. Cut it to shape, sand it smooth, and then rout a decorative edge and stain to suit.

Anchor it to the form board with self-starting wood screws driven from the back of the backboard. Place one screw at the top first, then stand back and check to make sure the backboard aligns properly with the edges of the mount. Then install a hanger.

If you decide not to use a backboard on the mount, you can simply

Finally, the hanger is installed. If you prefer, add a backboard, then a hanger.

install the hanger. For you convenience, any number of commercial hangers are available. Hold the mount up and determine the hanger location. This may be in the center, but in the case of offset mounts, the hanger location may be off-center. One method of determining the exact spot is to approximate the location and drive a temporary screw slightly into the back of the board. Then suspend the mount by the screw and see if it tilts to one side or the other. Adjust as needed until you find the proper hanger location.

Full-Body
and Other Mounts

As mentioned earlier, in addition to the usual head mounts, there are many other types you might want to try, including a variety of open-mouthed head mounts and full-body mounts in unusual poses.

15
Full-Body Mounts

A s you might guess, although the basic steps are much the same as for a head mount, a full-sized deer mount takes a great deal more time and effort. You may wish to tackle a smaller animal first, such as a squirrel, raccoon, fox or coyote, to practice on and learn from before you attempt a full-sized deer, especially a trophy buck.

MEASUREMENTS

The first step is to take a number of measurements as described in Section II, Chapter 4: all the head measurements, as well as a

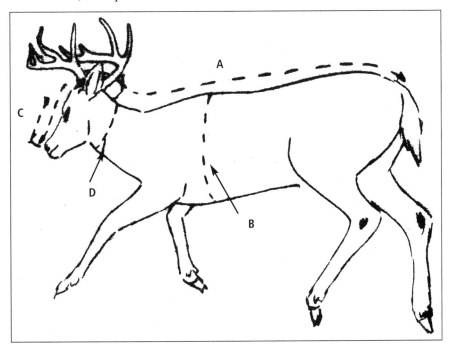

Full measurements are required before you can match the cape to a full-body form.

measurement from the end of the nose to the base of the tail and around the girth at the largest part of the belly. These measurements allow you to purchase the correct-size mount. Since there's a wide range of full-body forms available—standing, running, feeding, jumping and even lying down deer—reference photos of the animal are extremely important. This is especially true for the more unusual deer forms.

SKINNING

If mounting a full-body deer form, extreme care must be taken when skinning the entire body. The traditional method is much like an open-pelt for furs and other hides: A cut is made from the anus to just under the jaw and then a Y-cut is made in the top of the head (as

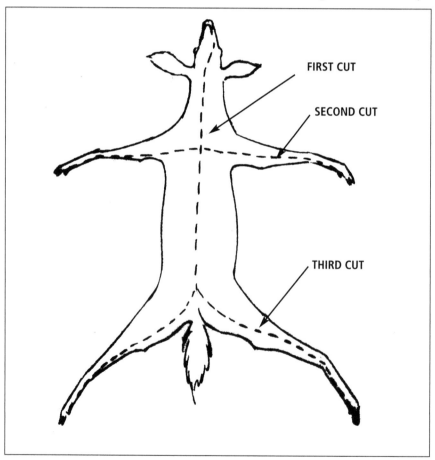

Skinning is in the open-case manner.

described in Section III, Chapter 5). An incision is made from the center-line cut along each leg down to the ankle bone. Start on the inside of the legs, turn and go around to the back and down to the ankle bone. Then make a final cut from the anus to the tip of the tail. Begin skinning at each ankle bone. When the enough skin is free, cut through the ankle bone and cut off the feet, leaving them attached to the skin.

Skinning then proceeds in the same manner as described for head capes: Carefully peel away the skin, cutting judiciously with a rounded-edge skinning knife to release the skin where needed. This method works especially well on mounts with lowered heads, such as a feeding-deer mount.

Many taxidermists prefer to make the underside cut just to the backside of the brisket. They stop the cut at the brisket and make the leg cuts from there. Finally, they make the small Y-cut on the top of the head. This method requires a bit more work to get the skin off the deer, but it provides a clean under-neck area that doesn't have to be sewn. When you reach the head, cut it off and cape it as described in Section III, Chapter 5.

An alternative method is to make one cut along the back, from the tip of the tail to the Y at the head. The skin is peeled down over the back with the leg skin left in the round, again cutting off the feet at the ankle joint and leaving them attached to the skin.

The skinning method you choose will depend mostly on how the animal is to be viewed, so that only the bare minimum amount of cut skin will ever be visible.

PRESERVING THE SKIN

As with the head mount, the next step is to flesh and clean the skin. With a full-body mount, of course, that involves quite a bit more effort. Without proper fleshing, the skin won't tan properly. Just take your time and make sure you do a thorough job: split the lips and carefully flesh the eyes and nose, just as you would with a head mount. The feet and ankles should also be cleaned down to the toes. The skin should then be salted, pickled, thinned and tanned, preferably with a quality tanning cream. Just make sure you get all parts of the skin treated in all steps.

PREPARING THE FORM

The form should be prepared in the same manner as for a head mount. Try-fit the skin in place on the manikin and make adjustments as necessary. If you have to remove material, use a rasp. You can add clay during the mounting process if the form needs to be slightly built up in some areas. Then make sure you roughen the form, sculpt the eyes and ears and, finally, add the antlers. As mentioned before, try-fit the skin as you go to make sure all fits properly.

MOUNTING

Mounting usually begins with the head. Apply a slow-working hide paste to the full body and slip the skin in place, pulling it into position over the entire body and checking to see that it fits and aligns with the form. Use pins to temporarily hold the skin in place and then begin sewing at the back of the head, making stitches about every one-quarter inch and keeping them pulled tight. Then tuck the eyes and nose.

If using the underbelly skinning cuts, go to the brisket and stitch to the belly. Pull the leg seams together, put the feet in the correct position and stitch the leg seams. Make sure to part the hairs and avoid pulling them into the stitches. Once you have the body sewn, go back to the face and complete it.

Some taxidermists prefer to work in the opposite way. First they determine the correct body position and pin the skin in place. Then they paste and work the face and head, followed by the pasting and stitching the remainder of the body.

Regardless of the method, add clay to muscling or to fill in where needed as you work. The skin may "drum" away from concave areas, in which case you'll need to drive in small nails or use pins to hold the skin in place. If you must stop overnight, cover the entire form with wet towels.

Once the skin is securely in position, brush it as needed, then use the flat of your hand to smooth out any problems. This also allows you to find any loose or drummed areas, which should be well pinned. Then allow the form to dry.

A full-body deer mount takes a great deal more work, expense and, of course, a bit more experience.

FINISHING

Finishing is basically the same as for a head mount, only with more body detail work. All seams should be well pounded down until they're flat and then the hair must be brushed and rebrushed over them. Painting will also include brightening the hoofs along with the head-mount paint finishing. Incidentally, deer testicle forms are also available for the full mounts.

16

Open-Mouth and
Other Head Mounts

The traditional closed-mouth style of taxidermy has been challenged these days by serious competition limited only by your imagination. Whether you want to work on a distinctive head mount or an unusual head on a full-body mount, manikins are available for just about any pose or mannerism, including open-mouth, deer browsing, fighting, Flehman or lip-curled bucks and even head-down rubbing mounts.

Open-mouth assemblies are available from the various suppliers. The assembly, with the tongue, is placed into the form and the lip skin is tucked in, around and under it. Note that in any open-mouthed mount, the mouth and tongue assembly will require detailed finish painting.

Open-mouth and more unusual style mounts can also be done with a little experience. Again, make sure you have good reference materials. (PHOTO COURTESY WASCO)

In unusual poses, it's extremely important to use eyes with a white scleral band around the outside and to make sure the eyes are set correctly so that they match the pose and are looking in the correct direction.

As you gain experience, you can tackle more complicated mounts such as the one shown by my friend Bob Ott.

One unusual mount has the deer showing aggression with the ears laid back and the head lowered.

Velvet mounts are extremely challenging. Products are available for curing the velvet, including Bollmann's Velvet Tan and Knobloch's Stop Slip, both available from WASCO.

Mule-deer mounts are done in basically the same manner as whitetails. Make sure you have good mule-deer references.

European and Antler Mounts

If you're looking for a less expensive, less time-consuming project, European and antler board mounts offer the perfect opportunity. Often chosen for lesser "trophies," such as a small spike or other "first" buck, they can also be used to display larger trophies, enhancing your collection when you don't wish to add a full mount.

17
European Mounts

Euuropean mount is a popular alternative to a full-skin mount—ideal for those not-so-great trophies you really don't want to spend a lot of time and money on. In their own right, they're quite attractive, with an unusual flair. European mounts are also quite easy to do, and they require less wall space and height than a full-shoulder mount.

SKINNING AND CLEANING

In most instances, the deer is first skinned down to the head, the head is removed from the carcass at the top of the spinal column and skinned out. The skinning process is basically the same as for caping, described in Section III, Chapter 5: Once you have the head completely skinned, remove the eyes and cut through the muscles on both sides of the lower jaw to detach it. Then cut off the tongue. Scrape and cut away as much meat and fat as possible from all portions of the head.

An excellent alternative to a head mount is a European mount. The example shown is mounted on a WASCO plaque especially designed for European mounts. (PHOTO COURTESY WASCO)

Place a large pot of water over a campfire, fish fryer or Coleman camp stove to provide the heat, and I might as well warn you: Finding a pot big enough to hold an antlered head can be a problem. Although the antlers should not be submerged or cooked, they are still awkward and make it hard to keep the head in the water. And since it's mighty hard to clean up afterwards—this is definitely an outside-only chore, not to be attempted on your kitchen stove—you definitely don't want to use your best soup-stock pot. I found that an old water-bath canner makes a great head-boiling pot (and I also use it for boiling traps, melting wax for defeathering water-fowl and other messy, outdoor chores).

Adding half a cup of baking soda or sal soda to the pot to help

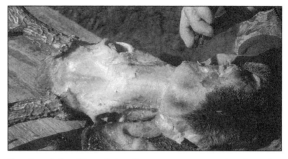

The head is skinned in the same manner, leaving the antlers attached. The lower jawbone is removed by cutting through the rear jaw muscles.

cut the grease during the cooking process, bring the water to a boil, then turn down the heat and simmer the head for several hours to soften the brains as well as the tissue remaining in and around the skull. The entire skull should be covered with water up to, but not above the antler bases. Keep adding hot water to maintain the correct water level around the head as the water evaporates.

When you remove the head from the pot, allow it to cool and then cut or peel off any meat, fat, muscle or membranes. As you pour out

The head is simmered to loosen all meat and other matter. The meat is then scraped and cut away, and the brain pan cleaned out with a wire coat hanger.

the water, check for pieces of bone or teeth that may have become loosened and fallen out in the cooking, which is not uncommon. Any teeth you find should be saved, as they can be glued back in place later. After you've removed all possible loosened meat and membranes, add fresh water, bring it to a full rolling boil and put the head back in the pot. Reduce the heat immediately and simmer the head for another couple of hours. Remove it from the water and cut or pick off any remaining meat, fat, muscle and membranes, using a small, flexible wire to clean out the tiny holes in the skull. Incidentally, you can quit working overnight between the two cooking phases, as long as the head is protected from pets and wild critters. But it's best to remove the meat while the head is still warm, because meat and muscles tend to become tougher as they cool. The hardest part of this entire chore is getting the brains out of the skull. It does take time, but make sure you remove every trace of brain matter. Just a tiny bit left can create quite a stench. After they're softened by boiling, the brains have to be literally picked and pulled out through the brain stem opening in the base of the skull. Commercial taxidermists use beetles to get the job done, but you can use a stiff wire, such as a coat hanger, to break up and pull out the gray matter. When you think you've successfully removed every bit of it, inspect the cavity with a flashlight to be sure and flush the interior with hot water several times to catch any pieces that might remain.

BLEACHING

To produce the popular ghost-white appearance, the skull must be thoroughly cleaned, inside and out, and bleached. Regular laundry

A combination of hairdresser's whitener and one-half forty-percent hydrogen peroxide is mixed and painted onto the skull, then covered with a plastic bag to bleach it out.

bleach should never be used because it tends to soften the bones of the skull, and common hydrogen peroxide isn't strong enough to do the chore. The best formula I've found is one-half hairdresser's whitener and one-half 40 percent hydrogen peroxide—both of which are available at your local beauty shop or beauty supply house.

Wearing rubber gloves and goggles, mix the ingredients in a plastic or glass (not metal) container and brush the mixture onto the skull. Seal the skull in a clear plastic bag and place the bag—with skull and antlers—on a white surface in direct sunlight. Make sure the skull is protected from pets and kids (and that kids and pets are protected from the skull), and allow it to work in the sun for several days. Then remove the bag and wash off the bleaching solution using a solution of one part vinegar to four parts water, which will stop the bleaching action. Wash the head thoroughly in clean, cold water.

MOUNTING

The European mount can be fastened to a plaque with screws from the back of the plaque, or you can use a special "slanted" European mount plaque to hold the skull in an "upright" position. You can also drill a hole below the brain stem opening and fasten the mount on a hook or picture frame hanger. Whatever you decide, once you discover how easy it is to make these, you'll probably end up doing several.

18
Antler-Board Mounts

An antler-board mount is another very popular way of displaying trophy antlers. Basically, it consists of antlers and skullcap fastened to a wooden plaque that allows them to be hung for display.

A number of commercial kits are available for this type of mount, providing the wooden mounting plaque, hanger, a base to cover the skullcap, then a decorative cover for the base and skullcap. A wide variety of these decorative covers are available in leather, formed plastic, flocked plastic and even metal. Foam antler-mount forms are also available; you just have to supply the covering material.

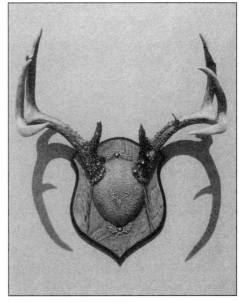

You can also make your own fairly easily. The first step is to cut off the antlers, leaving a small section of the skullcap attached to hold the antlers in place. Clean the skullcap of all hair, brain matter and flesh, then simmer it in hot water with a bit of baking soda to complete the cleaning. Remove it, wipe off

Antler mounts are also a very popular way of displaying trophies, and several different commercial kits are available. (PHOTO COURTESY WASCO)

all matter, and then flush the skullcap with cold, clean water.

Although wooden plaques are available, you can also make up your own fairly easily. Hardwoods, such as oak or walnut make the

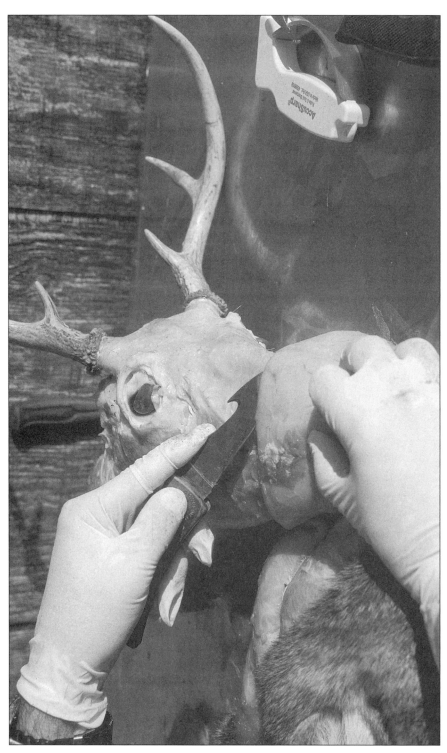

The skull is skinned. The skull cap cut away and then all hair and meat removed from the skull cap.

You can mount to a commercial plaque or create your own plaque.

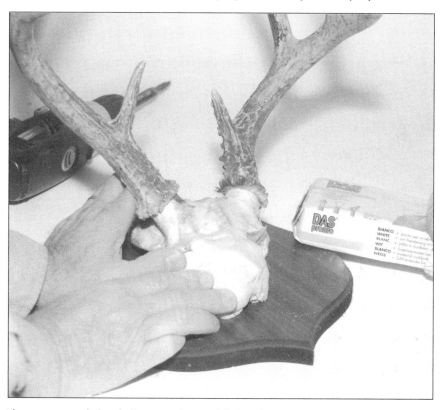

The area around the skullcap can be modeled with clay or papier-maché, and then covered with felt or leather held with decorative tacks.

best plaques. Cut to shape with a band saw, and then route the edges and sand smooth.

PAPIER-MÂCHÉ MOUNTS

Position the skullcap in place and fasten with self-starting wood screws through the skull into the plaque. (If you bore holes through it first, you'll avoid the risk of splitting out the skull with the screws.) Mix papier-mâché as per the instructions—it's readily available from taxidermy supply houses —and mold it around the skullcap to create a base. After the papier-mâché dries, shape and smooth it with sandpaper, then cover it with felt or leather and use decorative tacks around the material to hold it in place.

DO-IT-YOURSELF FOAM

You can create a base out of polyurethane foam, carving a chunk to fit around the antler bases or, better yet, forming one to fit by cutting a piece of 3/8-inch plywood in whatever shape you desire for the base. Attach the antlers to the plywood base with self-starting wood

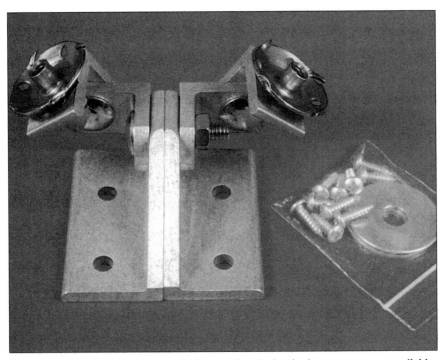

One unusual trophy is a mount made from antler sheds. Shed connectors are available for mounting the picked-up antlers to a plaque. (PHOTO COURTESY WASCO)

screws. Then, using cardboard, create a dam that encircles the wooden base and fasten it in place with staples. Tape off the antler burrs with masking or duct tape, mix two-part polyurethane foam (or use a spray-can of foam insulation) and pour or spray it into the cardboard dam. Make sure you have enough foam to create a raised section up to and around the antler bases. Once the foam sits up, use a rasp to carve it into a rounded, smooth shape and cover it with felt or lightweight leather, using staples to fasten the material on the back of the plywood. Then attach the form and antlers to a wooden plaque with screws from the back of the plaque into the plywood, and add the hanger to the back.

SHED ANTLERS

You can also create an unusual mount if you have a well-matched pair of sheds. Use shed-connectors, available from taxidermy supply houses. to anchor the sheds to the mounting board or plaque, then cover and finish as described above. It's a great way to display your scavenged trophies.

Novelty Deer Items

Over the years, creative taxidermists have found ways to make a number of unique items from deer "parts," including knife handles, gun and bow racks, lamps, sconces, and other novelties. These items offer great crafting opportunities and use up portions of the animal that might otherwise be wasted. They also add to the taxidermist's profits.

19

Leg and Foot Ornaments

D eer legs and feet can be skinned, tanned and mounted on wooden or plastic forms, available from taxidermist supply houses in straight leg (for use in lamps, candle stands and similar furnishings) or L-shaped for creating gun, bow and hat racks. You can buy ready made wooden plaques for the latter, as well as "rosettes" for finishing off around the ends of the legs. You can even buy artificial feet, which makes it easy to create your novelty even if all you have to work with are skins.

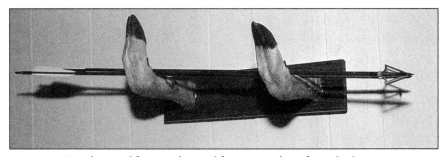

Deer legs and feet can be used for any number of novelty items.

SKINNING AND PRESERVING

To make any kind of foot ornament, the first step is to skin out the legs, cutting down the back of the each leg to the back of the hoof. Peel the hide down and off the leg until you reach the dewclaws. Cut through the dewclaw bones as close to the dewclaw itself as possible. Then continue peeling the skin down to the hooves. Use a rounded-point skinning knife to help release the skin as you go.

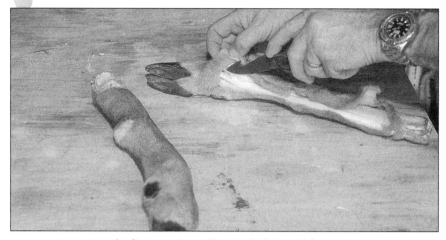

The first step is to skin out the legs and feet.

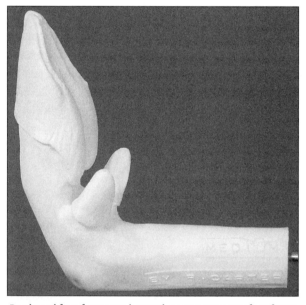

Purchased foot forms can be used, or you can carve foot forms from soft wood. (PHOTO COURTESY WASCO)

When you reach the hooves, stick the tip of a sharp-pointed knife down into the hooves and cut around them. Be patient. Skinning deer legs takes quite a bit of effort and time, but if you slip and cut through the skin, you have pretty well ruined it for the project. Sever all tendons and "break" the hooves off the bone. Again, be patient and careful; this also takes some effort.

Once the legs are skinned, spread out the skin and remove all the flesh from it and follow the traditional method of preserving it: Spread salt over the entire surface of the flesh side, working it in and around the dewclaws and hooves. Set the skin aside in a protected, dry place and allow the salt to cure and dry it—a process that usually takes about a week.

The skins are pickled and tanned, then mounted onto the forms and allowed to cure.

Pickling comes next. Bring one gallon of water to a boil and stir in 1/4 pound of borax and 1/4 pound of alum. Stir in 2-1/4 pounds of salt and keep stirring until all is dissolved, then allow it to cool. Pour the cooled-down solution into a plastic bucket or tub and immerse the skins. Leave them in the pickle bath for about a week, stirring several times each day.

Take the skins from the pickle bath and wash them in water with a cup of baking soda and a few drops of dishwashing detergent added. Rinse with clean, cold water until all soap is out and then allow the skins to drain for about half an hour. At this point, you can take a more modern approach and use a tanning cream to assure the skins are properly tanned.

MOUNTING

Perhaps you'd like to carve your own wooden forms from a soft wood, such as pine or basswood. In the case of L-shaped forms, a screw/bolt should be placed into the back of the forms, and they're available from woodworking supply houses. Footstool forms should have the screw/bolt in the top for anchoring to the stool frames. Of course, manufactured forms are also available from taxidermy supply houses.

Before mounting the feet/skins on the form, stuff taxidermist clay into the feet to hold them in place. Place the form inside the skin, adjusting by either sanding down or adding more clay to the form as needed to make a full and natural-looking foot. Starting at the foot, sew up the skin using a glover's needle and waxed linen thread or

Spiderwire fishing line. Leave the top flap open to let the skin to dry and cure in place, bearing in mind that the skin will shrink somewhat.

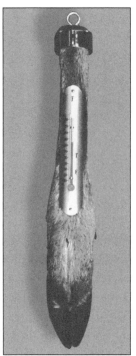

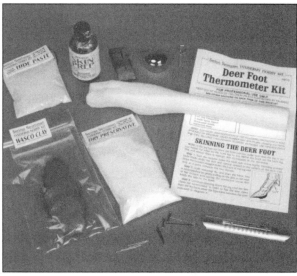

Other novelties include a thermometer holder made from a foot. (PHOTO COURTESY WASCO)
A kit with all the supplies needed and instructions makes this thermometer an easy project for beginners. (PHOTO COURTESY WASCO)

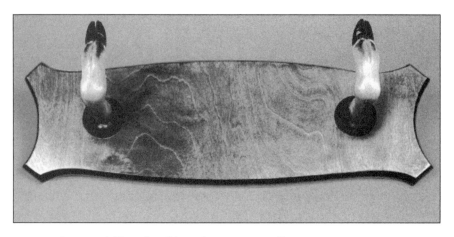

A gun-rack kit makes this project easy as well. (PHOTO COURTESY WASCO)

Deer legs can also be made into lamps with a lamp kit.
(PHOTO COURTESY WASCO)

Allow the legs to dry for approximately a week, then sand and polish the hooves to a nice glistening finish. Cut off the excess skin at the back of the leg. Bore bolt holes in the mounting boards and countersink in the back for the bolts and nuts. Then mount the legs to the board. FYI, deer legs used in lamps are fastened together using special lamps kits.

20
Other Deer Novelties

A variety of novelties can be made from other parts of the deer, including the antlers, various bones and the white rump skin or "flag."

DEER RUMPS

Deer rumps are an interesting novelty, very popular in hunting camps, and forms are available if you want to create these "fun" items. Basically, the rump is skinned, the tail opened and the

One of the more unusual novelties is a deer rump. A Deer Rump Kit comes with a special form and all supplies. (PHOTO COURTESY WASCO)

tail bone removed. The skin is fleshed, pickled and tanned, then glued to the form in the same manner as for a head mount.

ANTLER NOVELTIES

Shed antlers, smaller antlers that you may not desire to use for trophy mounts, as well as antlers that are broken or damaged can also have a number of uses. They can be cut into slices and used as knife handles, the tips can also be used as handles for knives as well as fireplace tools barbeque utensils. Solid antler sections can be made into door pulls, gate pulls and cabinet hardware. Antlers can be sliced into thin segments and used as buttons for clothing, belt buckles, hat-band sections, even pendants, bracelets, brooches and other jewelry.

Antlers can also be turned into a handy hunting tool: rattling antlers. Just cut off the tips and tie two together with a sturdy string for packing in and out. Make sure the tips are rounded so you won't

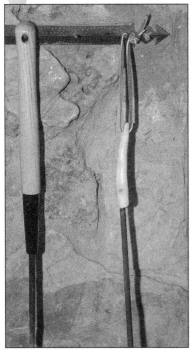 

Shed antlers and antlers not desired for trophy mounts can be used to create knife handles and for any number of other uses.

Antlers can also be used to create unusual lamps and decorative items

injure yourself should you fall on them.

If you have a lot of antlers, particularly sheds, consider using them in lamps and chandeliers. Arrange the antlers any way that pleases you, fasten them together with epoxy glue and run electrical wire through and around them to provide power for light bulbs. Or, for a simpler lodge light, use antlers as a decorative base for candles in glass holders.

JAWBONE PLAQUES

Among the more unusual deer novelties are jawbone display boards, which can be made up of different-age animals, with the ages marked. The boards can then be displayed at hunting lodges or clubs to help hunters and deer managers "age" animals that are taken and provide a good record for deer management purposes.

Making a jawbone plaque isn't complicated. After the head is skinned, remove the jawbone by cutting through the muscles at the back and on each side. (Note: Jawbones will split apart easily in the front where they are joined.) You'll only need one side for each plaque, but you might as well make up several while you're at it.

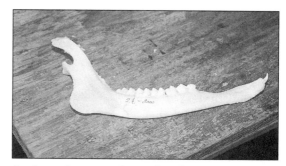

Jawbone plaques can be used to illustrate tooth aging of whitetails for lodges and hunting rooms.

Clean all flesh off the jawbone halves, then simmer them for a couple of hours to loosen the remainder of the flesh. Once the jawbone pieces are thoroughly clean, wash them in cold water. The jawbone can then be whitened just like a European mount, but be careful to brush the whitening agents onto the bone portion only and don't get it on the teeth. Once the bone is white, wash it thoroughly in clean, cold water and allow to dry. Use the age-determining charts you'll find in any number of wildlife management books as a reference and write the age on the side of the jawbone with a fine-line felt-tip pen. Then glue the jawbones to an attractive wooden plaque and coat both the jawbones and the plaque with a good gloss varnish.

DEER SKINS

If using European and antler-board mount systems, the whole skin is often left over, and if properly tanned, can be turned into very useful items. These skins can be tanned hair-on for robes and wall hangings, or hair-off for clothing, footwear and leather accessories.

If the skins are to be tanned hair on, they are basically treated in the same way modern capes are tanned, as described in Section IV, Chapter 9. The skins should be well fleshed, salted, pickled,

The hides or skins can also be tanned and used for robes, hangings, or even for clothing and accessories.

thinned, then tanned using a tanning agent specified for leather work, such as Rittel's EZ-2000 and the Deer Hunter's Hide Tanning Formula.

Skins may be tanned with hair on.

The main difference is that the skins must be "broken" or made flexible, which does take a bit of work and time. You need to work them over a breaking beam as they dry so they don't get completely dry and hard. They are then often oiled to keep them further softened.

Removing the hair for hair-off hides is a fairly easy but messy step. The skins are first soaked in a solution of lime water with one cup of hydrated builder's or fine agricultural lime added per gallon of water. Weight the skins down so they don't "float" up and out of the solution and allow them to stay in the lime water for about a week. Stir occasionally to make sure the liquid reaches all parts of the skin evenly. The hair-loosening process could even take a couple of weeks, depending on temperature and humidity.

From time to time, remove the skin and, wearing rubber gloves, pull on the hair. When it slips out easily, it's ready to work. Place the skin over a fleshing beam or large log and, still wearing rubber gloves plus long pants, a long-sleeved shirt, a

Or the hair may be removed.

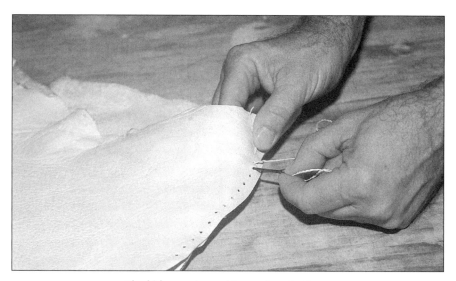

The hides are tanned to produce leather.

rubber apron and eye protection, use. a large hunting knife held perpendicular to the skin, a drawknife or better yet a fleshing knife to scrape away the hair. It should come off fairly easily. When you finish the chore, go over the entire hide again to make sure all the upper membrane is removed. Then salt, pickle and tan as before, and you're ready to make shirts, pants, footwear, belts and other accessories from the resulting leather. Clearly, if you're already tanning capes, adding extra skins to the pickling and tanning solutions can make your taxidermy work very lucrative.

Mount Maintenance and Repair

With proper mounting procedures, mounted deer heads are relatively easy to care for. Deer head mounts do, however, require periodic maintenance.

21
Cleaning and Refinishing

D ust, smoke, and lint naturally collect on mounts, and the simplest maintenance step you can take is regular dusting, twice a year at the very least as part of your usual spring and fall cleaning. Use a feather duster or one of the modern anti-static devices.

If the mount is not easily reachable, take it off the wall and put it on the floor or a table for dusting, being careful to handle it by the nose and base only without "ruffling" the hair. You can use a portable hand vacuum or a larger adjustable machine on light-suction mode to remove accumula-tions of dirt, smoke and dust. Always

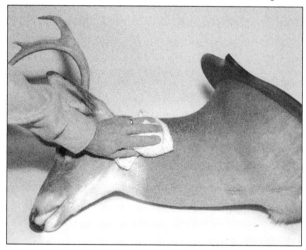

An occasional cleaning is usually all that's required for modern-day mounts. Older mounts may need refurbishing using a commercial mount cleaner.

go with the hair when vacuuming or rubbing in any manner, and use caution around the eyes so as not to break lashes. Once you've finished vacuuming, use a brush to lightly fluff the hair, and then brush it back smooth. Unruly hairs can be held in place with hair gel, brushing any excess away after the gel has set.

Deer heads that are extremely grimy can also be washed down after vacuuming. Use a soft cloth or sponge and warm water to which you've added a mild dishingwashing soap and a teaspoon of household ammonia. Always wash with the direction of the hair, beginning with the nose, mouth and chin and working up the face toward the ears and then down the neck. Scrub the water into the hairs with a soft brush and then rinse thoroughly to get out all the soap. Finally, brush in the direction of the hair to smooth the surface and allow the mount to air dry, outside if possible.

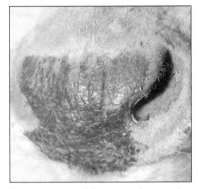

Eyes, noses, and lips may also require repainting and brightening.

For maximum ease and convenience, you can use one of today's specially formulated foamless mount cleaners, such as Mount Brite from WASCO. This product brightens and conditions new mounts and both cleans and restores old mounts—even those long neglected, with years of smoke and dust accumulation. You simply apply Mount Brite with a paintbrush or soft cloth, blot dry and wipe down with another dry cloth, going with the direction of the hair. Allow the mount to dry completely—the cleaner leaves no residue—then smooth it down with a soft-bristle brush.

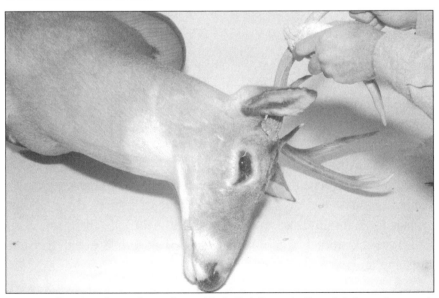

Occasionally wipe down the antlers with boiled linseed oil to brighten them and prevent them from drying out.

Use a soft tissue or cotton swabs and glass cleaner to clean and brighten the eyes, and apply a bit of light oil to the nose, wiping off any excess. You can put a bit of furniture oil or boiled linseed oil on a soft cloth and use it to polish the antlers. And if the antlers have become bleached through the years, you can buy antler stain to darken them.

REFINISHING

Quite often the nose, lips and the area around the eyes will dry out, or the paint will become cracked. If that's the case, repaint using artist's oil colors or Sallie Dahmes Finishing Wax and use a polyurethane varnish to add gloss to the

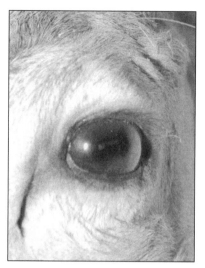

Loose or cracked portions can sometimes be repaired by injecting glue under the skin and pinning the skin back in place. This often happens around the eyes.

nose after the paint dries. If the hide is loosening or "drumming" away from the form, a common problem, inject a thin solution of glue into the area and apply a suitable clamp to hold the hide in place until the glue dries.

SOURCES

The following companies carry a full line of whitetail mount supplies.

Wildlife Artist Supply Company (WASCO)
1-800-334-8012 • *www.taxidermy.com*

Van Dykes
1-800-843-3320 • *vandykestaxidermy.com*

John Rinehart Taxidermy Supply Company (a McKenzie Company)
1-800-279-7985 • *www.mckenziesp.com*

McKenzie Taxidermy Supply
1-800-279-7985 • *www.mckenziesp.com*

Precision Mannikins, (a McKenzie Company)
1-800-279-7985 • *www.mckenziesp.com*

Buckeye Mannikins, (a McKenzie Company)
1-800-279-7985 • *www.mckenziesp.com*

Rayline Mannikins, Inc., (a McKenzie Company)
1-800-279-7985 • *www.mckenziesp.com*

WOODS N' WATER
PRESS

Other Outdoorsman's Edge Books Available From
Woods N' Water Press

TO ORDER,
Call us at 1-800-652-7527, write, to us at Woods N' Water Press, P.O. Box 550, Florida, NY 10921 or visit us on the web at *www.fiduccia.com* or *www.outdoorsmansedge.com.*